18 TO 80

A Simple and Practical Guide to
Money and Retirement for all Ages

Published by Modern Growth Press in San Antonio, TX.

ISBN 978-1-948209-99-1 (Audio)
ISBN 978-1-948209-98-4 (Paperback)
ISBN 978-1-948209-97-7 (EBook)

Cover Design by: Rojo032

Editing by Michelle Booth

Book design by Jean Boles
jean.bolesbooks@gmail.com

While the author has made every effort to provide accurate telephone numbers and Internet addresses at the time of publication, neither the publisher nor the author assumes any responsibility for errors, or for changes that occur after publication. Further, publisher does not have any control over and does not assume any responsibility for third party Web sites or their content.

Printed in the United States of America

Hypothetical examples provided are for illustrative purposes only and are not intended to represent the past or future performance of any specific investment.

Darryl W. Lyons

If you pass this book along to a friend or family member, this is the place to give them a note of encouragement.

If you need resources and advice beyond the content of the book, please visit Darryl's website:

www.PAXFinancialGroup.com

PAX™

Financial Group, LLC

To My Caresse

CONTENTS

Preface

I slammed the door as I exited the black Isuzu Rodeo. I was frustrated with my bank account. I just signed the Isuzu lease and was struggling to make the first payment. Buyer's remorse sat on the front seat beside me.

Committed to a commission-only job selling financial products, I was way off the quota. If I didn't convince someone soon to buy, my probation would end and I'd be canned. I wasn't even close to quota and had been verbally warned.

I sighed deeply as I walked around the front side of the SUV. I stepped over the curb and opened the door to the office located in a large chalky-white industrial office complex. Yes, there was a red and black "no solicitor" sign plastered to the door. I admit, I pretended not to see it. If an assertive gatekeeper called me out on my violation, I had a prepared remark to overcome my disrespect. My desperation for a paying customer was worth the risk.

There was no gatekeeper at the front desk of the home health agency. It was clean and eerily quiet for a successful small business. I heard some paper shuffling so I looped around the corner, made my way through the hallway and found a middle-aged man in a small office, surrounded by boxes, diligently crunching numbers. He woke up from his numbers trance like he hadn't seen another face in a few days. "Come on in!" he said. I was relieved by his friendliness.

We exchanged pleasantries as I quickly assessed his memorabilia, pictures, and paintings in search of a common ground. Then, he asserted, "What are you selling?" I framed my pitch for investments, insurance, and financial planning and threw out as many words and phrases so that one of them might stick. He looked at me crookedly, paused, and responded, "Well, me and my business partner need some life insurance. Can you sell us some?"

"Of course!" I said. Now, keep in mind, I had been sweating all day in the Texas summer sun. My only suit was ridiculously wrinkled. This business owner knew intuitively my journey, and I'm sure he felt a little sorry for me. But at this point, pity could be a paycheck, so I'll take it.

Unfortunately, he gave me only verbal interest. He wasn't in a rush into buying life insurance . . . who is anyway? He needed time to do some homework and figure out how much coverage they needed. In the meantime, I held on to hope.

So, while impatiently waiting, week in and week out, in the Texas heat, I continued to knock on doors. Every day. Every. Single. Day. I drove across the state down county roads pitching to ranch hands and farmers. I rang doorbells in neighborhoods and interrupted grandmas watching Oprah. I disturbed night-shift workers by banging on screen doors of trailer parks. I drove across the city soliciting everyone from the poor in the projects to the rich in the high rises.

I tried to be efficient with my time and I studied my financial planning note cards at every stop light or stop sign.

My biggest issue with my pursuit of paying customers was fuel. When my gas gauge would light up, I would often turn off the AC to make my Rodeo roll a little farther. On more than one occasion, I had to stop by a pawn shop and drop off my college class ring to pay for the gas needed to continue my ambition. The irony is that despite being broke, I was desperate to help people with money. I felt, I guess you might say, that I had a calling.

Then, the middle-aged home health guy called.

He and his partner agreed to give me a shot and allowed me to sell them a large life insurance policy. As an unexpected bonus, they asked me to set up a company 401(k) plan. I'll never forget my hands literally trembling when we signed the agreements.

I narrowly escaped from being fired. I survived and I was injected with optimism and hope. Not only did I survive, but I had the renewed energy of experiencing what it's like to help someone with their money.

Today, I have elevated from broke into financial comfort. Because of my journey, I passionately do my best to provide money direction to thousands of people every day. I chat money with politicians on Capitol Hill, senior pastors of churches, CEOs, local news stations, international organizations, and (very proudly) moms and dads looking for a fair shake.

I received a thoughtful question from one of the dads the other day. He asked, "On a scale of one to ten how important is money to you?" I had to think about this one because my reply could come out wrong.

"Well," I answered, "Let's look at history. Whether you think the Bible is a history book or if you think it's the word of God, the truth is that the book contains 2,350 references to money. Money is referenced more than the words faith and prayer . . . combined. So, if we know anything about human history, money has and will always be important. Is it important to me? Yes, and it's important to you as well. Sometimes we just don't admit it."

The reason money is so important is that if it is mismanaged, misplaced, or misunderstood then it will assist in divorce, broken relationships, and poverty.

My interest in money is because of the way it impacts families in the community. I want to help others make a few adjustments to their current money approach. Today, I'm asking you to make a few adjustments. Today, I'm knocking on your door.

Introduction to The Middle Class

What do you call a billionaire who has blown through three marriages and has estranged kids? A success. At least that's what the headlines of the *Wall Street Journal* and *People* declare. At first glance, the cover image of a wealthy billionaire standing between his cherry red convertible and limited edition Tundra jolts feelings of jealousy, envy, or maybe even regret.

Those of us in the middle class, who hold firmly to family values, digest the story beyond the headline and are thankful for the life we've been given.

But here's the crux . . .

We can't let our wallets be influenced so easily. Now, more than ever, middle-class money is tight. On the opposite page is a typical middle-class budget in America today.

Gross Monthly Income	**$ 6,250**
Federal Income Taxes	$ (938)
Social Security Taxes	$ (391)
Medicare Taxes	$ (91)
401k Contribution	$ (938)
Health Insurance	$ (650)
Net Monthly Paycheck	**$ 3,244**
Mortgage	$ (1,500)
Car Payment	$ (400)
Car Payment	$ (400)
Credit Card	$ (100)
Utilities	$ (150)
Cellphone	$ (100)
Groceries	$ (600)
Cash Flow after bills	**$ (6)**

Where is the money for braces, gymnastics, birthday gifts, summer camps, and school supplies? *It's gone.*

So, who is middle class?

The US Commerce Department defined "middle class in America" in a 2010 report this way . . . "aspirations for homeownership, a car for each adult, health security, a college education for each child, retirement security, and a family vacation each year." So, if you have those aspirations, you may be middle class.

I would suggest that middle class is when you don't have the government paying for your food but you don't own a yacht either. It's somewhere in between.

The middle-class people I thought of when I wrote this book can afford Christmas yet put limits on holiday spending. We can afford a car so long as we put "pen to paper" on financing and purchasing options. Some have suffered divorce, others are widows. Many made sacrifices to send kids to college. We have a retirement dream but know that one mini money mistake drowns the dream.

We are willing to fight for a fair shake and leave the world better than we found it.

We are the middle class.

How To Read This Book

"**G**etting waaarmer," replies the playful five-year-old as her little sister searches for the hidden toy. The same temperature progression occurs as we get one step closer to retirement every year we blow out the candles. The reason we as a country are so infatuated with retirement is because of two possible outcomes. One is we retire broke, unhealthy, and a burden to others. This is a frightening reality for many Americans. The other, more blissful outlook is retiring with a bucket full of money allowing you to wake up without an alarm at the coastline of your choosing. I desire the latter and I know you do as well.

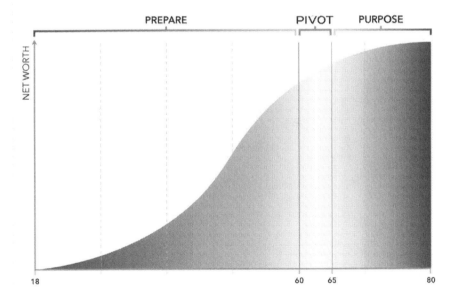

The format of this book is divided into three sections. The first section is PREPARE. It begins with age eighteen when someone is far away from and "cold" relative to retirement. Each year they get a little warmer as they approach retirement. In the PREPARE section, you will be executing one action item each year that will dramatically increase the chance of a successful retirement. If you are bit older, share this section of the book with your kids. It has just enough nuggets of money talk to get them moving in the right direction.

This next section is very warm and moving into hot. This section starts at age sixty and is called PIVOT. Because I don't believe in retirement (more on this to come), I prefer that you PIVOT into the next chapter of your life. The PIVOT section will discuss a five-year transition as you straddle between employment and retirement life. Our financial conversation will become a little more detailed here as we can't afford to make mistakes at this age in life.

The final section is the red-hot PURPOSE section and kicks off right at retirement, which for many people is at age sixty-five. In this section we will discuss how critical purpose is to your life and the threats that could prevent you from leaving the legacy you intended to leave. If you are younger, you will want to share this section with your parents. There are a lot of threats that need to be addressed as age often prevents second chances.

I want you to feel comfortable jumping strait to the section with your age and moving on from there. You are not obligated to start sooner, but you might consider going back to double check your progress. Also, looking twenty more years in your money future will provide the insight into the threats that might exist not only in your life but in your parents' financial life as well. Regardless, don't be concerned about reading every year. This content is to help you win with money so you can PIVOT with PURPOSE. Let it be your guide as you make the important money adjustments to not only reduce stress, but to actually win.

One more heads up . . . the book is not always written in order of priorities. It is formatted, through thousands of money conversations, to discuss money issues on your mind at your particular age. I hope to have met you where you are.

Keep in mind that this book is full of heuristics (rules of thumbs) to allow you to grasp an idea and then apply it based on your own situation. Much of this content is derived from a relatively new study called "Behavioral Finance." Yet, I'll skip the words amygdala and dopamine and get practical with money. This book is a culmination of over twenty years of thinking, research, and personal kneecap-to-kneecap conversations with thousands of middle-class folks trying to get a fair shake.

At the end of each decade, I'll provide you with a quick summary called, "Done in a Decade." It will include the action items that should have been done over the prior decade. If they haven't been accomplished . . . no worries! You are not alone. Just start making the changes now. Like they say, the best time to plant a tree was twenty years ago. When is the second best time? Today. Don't dwell in the "if onlys" of the past or the "what ifs" of the future. Just start making one money change at a time. I know that your PIVOT will be much better than you would have ever imagined.

SECTION I: PREPARE

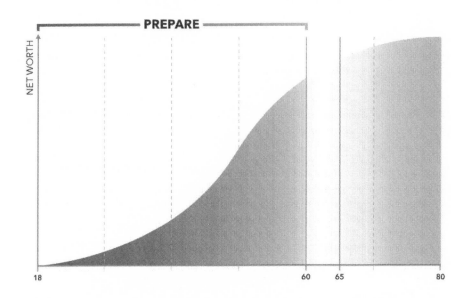

PREPARE is the long season in life before retirement age. We have to acknowledge, with maturity, that at some point in the future our minds and our bodies might not work the same. At age sixty-five, if we haven't saved a pile of cash and our bodies break down, we'll spend twenty years (from age sixty-five to age eighty-five) as money burdens for our children. This is a real reverse-generational transfer of wealth.

That is why we have to be smart and disciplined with money . . . NOW. This is an uphill battle in America. We are fighting to hold on to our wallets and purses against our neighbor's influence and "one-click" Amazon purchases that tempt us daily.

In this section we will discuss how challenging it is to overcome the subconscious decision-making that impacts our ability to save over time.

It is not impossible. I have seen individuals push aside American consumerism. Jason and Kim made a commitment to drive eighteen-wheelers across the country to be debt free, and accumulated more wealth than attorneys and doctors. Chuck and Erica decided to deliver pizzas to get financially right despite having advanced educations and full-time leadership careers. Don paid off his house by age forty with only a modest income. There are many stories of families who get focused and stiff-arm American consumerism and the pressure to spend.

Recognizing the threats and our own personal weaknesses are key character qualities when accumulating wealth. As an example, if you want to eat out, but are on a budget, then drink water and commit to split the meal with your spouse. Or, if you tend to spend everything you make, then force yourself to save 15 percent before your paycheck ever hits your bank account.

In this PREPARE section, from age eighteen to age fifty-nine, we will unpack the most salient financial issues and the necessary strategies to implement money disciplines for the benefit of you, others, and your future self.

Age 18: The Pause

"I'm not married, I frequently use my debit card to buy things that cost less than three dollars, and my bedroom is so untidy it looks like vandals ransacked the Anthropologie sale section. I'm kind of a mess."

— Mindy Kaling, actress

I hate to admit it, but I do like to buy stuff. I can always find a reason to buy new sneakers, new music, technology, watches, an iPhone case, headphones, socks, or concert tickets. My purchase is always proceeded by the words, "Oh, that's pretty cool."

You know this.

It is so easy to buy today. Back in the day, you would have to break a twenty to buy something.

McDonald's loves that you don't have to break a twenty anymore. In fact, today McDonald's is making $3.50 more for each transaction compared to the time in our lives when cash was predominantly used. Considering they sell seventy-five burgers every second, that's a lot of extra cash!

If McDonald's knows that easy purchase options are money makers, so does every store in a mall or outlet and I can assure you that Amazon knows the game as well.

Today, debit cards, "one-click pay," watches, smartphones, and thumbprint purchases all take away the necessary "pause" in spending that allows us time to think. It's a MasterCard mental hijack and it steals directly from your wallet.

The research is clear: when there is less friction to buying, you will spend more.

Develop a habit to simply pause before you buy. The bigger the purchase, the longer the pause. I had a friend who decided to get a night's rest before purchasing a new truck. This one night of rational thinking prevented him from absorbing an $800 monthly truck payment. The pause is powerful to building wealth. That's why I wanted to introduce it to you early in life.

If you need help pausing, ask yourself, "Do I need it, do I love it, or will it make me money?" (The last question is for the entrepreneur.) If you can't answer the questions with an affirmative, walk away from Amazon or track out of Target. Your product will be there tomorrow.

Finally, I want to make sure you also implement the following rules that will protect you in your spending journey.

1. Get alerts from your bank. You can set up alerts with most banks that notify you if your account falls below a certain balance. This will help you avoid dreaded overdraft fees.

2. Sign up for a money tracker program. There are plenty of options available such as Dave Ramsey's Every Dollar, Quicken, and Mint.com. Don't expect the software to do all the work; you have to input data and stop spending when you are about to run short of money. Start by checking on your spending at least every month to make course corrections before it's too late.

3. Never use credit cards or department store cards. I don't care what points, discounts, or free offers are pitched by the clerk. They are dangerous.

What if you had just enough pauses in your spending that you were able to save up for a car? It is possible. But your new ride can be expensive if you don't buy it the right way. This car purchase is the topic of our next chapter.

Age 19: Don't Fall For Financing

"Before someone gets their driver's license they should have to beat Rainbow Road on Mario Kart without falling off."

—Unknown

Do millionaires buy used or new cars?

Before I answer that question, let me provide some background information . . .

First, let's digest how most (non-millionaires) buy cars . . . Kelley Blue Book reports that the average new car transaction price is $33,340.

If someone decides to finance a $33,340 shiny new car, then about $600 will be sucked out of their bank account each month.

There is a premium to pay for all the safety features, technology, and gadgets added to cars each year. Sometimes I miss my 1984 GMC pickup where I could find the parts under the hood and tinker with the V8 to make the clicking sound stop. Now, you need an advanced degree in computer science to uncover and work on your vehicle. Today's cars are complex . . . and that complexity comes with a price. But, let's not let the multitude of features force us into overpaying.

As a starting rule of thumb, if you currently have a car payment of over 15 percent of your take-home pay you are paying too much. If you have car payments beyond four years, you are paying for too long. The ideal and realistic goal for everyone is to avoid the dreaded car payment altogether.

Don't be too proud. Buy a beater and pay cash.

You do not need to be Matthew McConaughey contemplating life in a Lincoln to be successful. If you fall for this marketing trick, you will fall for financing. The car financing trap becomes a habit and is repeated every four years of life.

Later, when you have a family, you'll end up with a couple of $33,000 SUVs. At that time, you'll need to figure out how to pay $1,200 in car payments due on the fifteenth of every month.

This cycle happens all the time and it begins with the first car purchase. So don't fall for the car financing trap. Think like a millionaire: buy used and pay with cash.

To answer the above question that started the conversation . . . according to Thomas J. Stanley, author of the best seller *Millionaire Next Door*, only 23.5 percent of millionaires purchase a *new* car.

Is your car paid off? Way to go!

Now, the ideal and normal life with a substantial paycheck and predictable expenses doesn't exist. You need to have set aside some cash for life's uncertainties. This next chapter is about helping you not go into freak-out mode when a huge bill shows up in your mailbox.

Age 20: Normal Is Only A Washing Machine Setting

"An emergency fund turns a crisis into an inconvenience."

—Dave Ramsey, *New York Times* best-selling author

Have you ever been in a car accident? Had an emergency medical issue? Have you had both at the same time? I did. I was hit by an uninsured motorist and sustained a painful neck injury. To top it off, I didn't have much cash in the bank. This could happen to me again or it could happen to you.

You may have the impression that life will turn out to be financially perfect. You get a job, the paycheck hits your bank account, you spend the money, and life progresses. However, this isn't normal. The reality is that life happens and when it does there is a price tag with it. We call this price tag emergencies.

Pew published a survey on American finances and six out of ten Americans said they suffered some sort of "economic shock" in the prior twelve months.

I know we think of emergencies as spontaneous road trips or an "unexpected" birthday gift for a twenty-five-year-old cousin, but the emergency fund is set up for true emergencies: the inevitable job loss and expensive medical bills.

(a) Job Loss

It is a painful journey in today's marketplace for someone hunting for work. Face it . . . the implementation of automation has changed the skill set required to justify the high cost of wages, social security, and unemployment insurance most employers have to consider

24

when making a hiring decision. Consider this: most people who get laid off need four months to find work. Can you survive right now without a paycheck for four months?

(b) Medical Bills

With the Affordable Care Act (ACA) much of the initial financial burden for health care is on your shoulders. Before insurance pays, you will have to cover the deductible. Today, the average deductible for an individual is $1,318. But when you tack on the other out-of-pocket costs such as co-insurance, you will be paying much more than that.

Also, check your policy's maximum out-of-pocket costs. For the 2017 plan year, the out-of-pocket limit for a marketplace plan was $7,150 for an individual plan and $14,300 for a family plan. As I said, few of us have the cash to cover these medical costs.

An emergency fund is called a *rainy day fund* because when the unexpected storm comes you will not be worried like those who didn't prepare. Establish an emergency fund between three and six times your monthly expenses.

In the next chapter, I will share with you a cool strategy to help you pay for upcoming non-emergency expenses.

Age 21: Save To Spend

"The way you spend Christmas is far more important than how much."

— **Henry David Thoreau, American poet and philosopher**

We all know that long-term saving is critical to financial success, but first we have to get our short-term (within the year) saving right. We have to develop a habit of setting aside some of our paycheck for upcoming annual expenses . . . like Christmas.

According to a survey conducted by Magnify Money, the average American racks up about $1,000 in debt over Christmas.

In the retail world, this is the Super Bowl. Marketers come with a plan, and consumers come ill-prepared. For example, one appliance store pumped in the smell of apple pie, and the sale of ovens and fridges went up 23 percent. As another example, some companies will give you free chocolate because it increases your desire for nonfood luxury items right after you enjoy the treat. Retailers are marketing pros; you need to be prepared for the game.

During the holidays we see the most careless collision of emotion and money . . . and Walmart knows it. The truth is that emotions and money just don't mix.

Below are three steps to help you "save to spend" for Christmas . . .

First, calculate your current spending. Set some time aside (probably around twenty minutes) and add up all the December spending associated with Christmas. Add up the gifts, the dining out, the holiday parties, the events you hosted, the clothes, the food, and anything else red and green. Let's assume the number comes up to $1,000.

Next, add fluff room. Saving to spend is always a little more than you originally thought. Go ahead and add 25 percent to your total. In our example this would be $1,000 X 1.25% = $1,250.

Finally, divide and save. Take the $1,250 and divide it by twelve. This is the monthly amount you will set aside to prepare for next year's holiday season. I have done this for years and . . . it works. You can put the monthly allotment in a savings account with the bank or you can place it in an envelope hidden in your home. In our example, you will need to set aside just over $100 per month.

Once you get saving to spend down for Christmas, this strategy should be applied toward a car purchase, vacations, and other future purchases. It begins with good, mature money habits.

Enjoy Christmas, but know that while you are on the ladder hanging Christmas lights there really are children scared, hungry, and alone. In the next chapter, I'll share with you the impact that giving to those who are hurting and hungry has on your own life. It really is remarkable.

Age 22: You Gotta Give

"No one has ever become poor by giving."

— The Diary of Anne Frank

According to *Giving USA 2016,* the Annual Report on Philanthropy, Americans give around 2 percent of their income to charity or other nonprofit organizations.

Does this strike you as a low number?

If I suggested that our debit card reflects our heart, then it is safe to say that we care . . . just a little. We care about 2 percent.

Outside of the real, painful, global needs, there are interpersonal reasons why it's critical to consistently commit to giving now.

First, givers are happier.

According to the Science of Generosity Initiative at Notre Dame, those who gave more than 10 percent of their income say they rarely or never experience depression compared to those who don't give 10 percent. Many Americans suffer from depression and much of the depression and/or anxiety is triggered because of money problems. The irony is that you may be able to solve your money problems by giving away more money.

I would suggest that a money/depression correlation is so tight that one might conclude that giving away more money could actually reduce depression. I don't think it's a stretch to suggest that by giving money, potentially reducing depression, you will think more clearly. When you think more clearly, you make better money decisions, thereby turning around your financial life.

Second, givers have perspective.

Whenever you give regularly you receive newsletters and emails keeping you abreast of the charity. There will be powerful and inspirational stories in these newsletters that will deliver perspective. Those stories will minimize your first-world, trivial money concerns. It is possible that right now, your current perspective is tainted. Your only point of reference is a friend's wardrobe or your college buddy's promotion. This point of reference is a Western fallacy that traps us in consumerism and worry.

John D. Rockefeller's mother forced him to give 10 percent of his income as a child and he never quit. Eventually he became the wealthiest man in America. He even said, "I never would have been able to tithe the first million dollars I ever made if I had not tithed my first salary, which was $1.50 per week."

Whether you have a little or a lot, giving is good for others and possibly even better for you. When we're honest with ourselves, there really isn't a good excuse not to consistently give. We just need to stop drinking beer, reduce the Starbucks, or dine out less.

Having trouble getting started? Begin to give where you are involved, like your local church or neighborhood where you can celebrate the results and progress. Then, expand your giving beyond those closest to you. You'll be shocked at the number of people who care about what you care about.

Age 23: Disciplined Saving

"You can be young without money, but you can't be old without it."

— Tennessee Williams, playwright

The Center for Retirement Research at Boston College conducted a study and suggested that individuals with average wages need to save 15 percent of their income. This is of course the general rule of thumb and doesn't always translate to your specific goals. For example, you may want to retire early. You may want a larger retirement check. You may want to exclude social security in your planning assumptions. Those factors would turn the 15 percent dial one way or another.

But let's assume you don't have time or energy to digest the details, and you are going to own the 15 percent as your personal game plan. Hey, you've got to start somewhere right?

You do the math and pencil down your gross paycheck (before any taxes and deductions) and multiply it by 15 percent. Then, reality sets in. You don't have much left if you're forced to save this 15 percent number.

Here's what you do . . .

First, you have to get rid of some of those monthly bank drafts. Take notice of how many companies love your commitment to monthly billing. The reason Netflix and Sprint are in love with drafting your bank account is that we set it and forget it. Companies even give you a free trial to tap into a subconscious purchasing behavior called loss aversion.

Next, start with saving a minimum of 10 percent. Don't settle for less than this number as your starting point. You have to get going now and the amount needs to be significant. Also, don't count your company match because they could yank that away in any given year if your employer gets in a cash crunch.

Finally, you have to commit to increase your retirement savings by 1 percent. Increase your contribution by 1 percent every year at open enrollment. In five years you'll be at 15 percent and you won't even feel it. Some 401(k) experts have been so impressed by the science behind automatic contribution escalations they have installed features that will do it for you. Check with your plan administrator.

I know you may have to sacrifice a few lattes and after-hours drinks. Don't listen to the foolish and broke who preach, "Well, you only live once." In the end, they will be poor and you won't.

Get in a rhythm of saving for retirement. It takes a few years, but you'll be proud when you see the money add up. Now, in order to put even more money away, you'll need to get a pay raise. In the next chapter, I'll share an evidence-based approach to improve your performance so your boss is utterly compelled to pay you more.

> *I graduated college from a private university with over $30,000 in student loans. I was making peanuts at the start of my career and could barely afford the student-loan payment. Often, I would call the lender and ask if I could skip some payments because I was broke. It was difficult. But I threw all extra money I could muster toward repaying the loan. Tax refunds, bonuses, commissions, and other little windfalls went toward the student-loan balance. It took some time and discipline. But, I finally paid it off. It feels good today not worrying about a pesky student-loan payment. I know you can knock them out as well. Just stay focused. A student-loan-free life is refreshing.*

Age 24: What Your Boss Really Wants

"Opportunity is missed by people because it is dressed in overalls and looks like work."

—Thomas Edison, American inventor

Today, there is a chasm of expectations between young hires who want fast money and employers who want long-term leaders. At the risk of overgeneralizing, young hires have an unrealistic expectation of rapid advancement and accelerated compensation. Alternatively, employers take a prolonged period of time to accurately assess the skills and establish a long-term dollar value to those skills. Employers want to see effective, responsible leaders who bring value to the organization.

While the employer is in the evaluation period, a young employee can display signs of frustration. "When am I going to get a raise?" "When am I getting promoted?" "Why are others getting benefits that I'm not?" This attitude, whether expressed or subconscious, is the beginning of the decline in the employee/employer relationship.

Check this out future high-income earners . . . employers are seeking qualities of leadership that take a considerable amount of time and various stress tests to assess.

According to the National Association of Colleges and Employers, 80.1 percent of employers said they are looking for evidence of leadership skills. Leadership engulfs the other skills of computer navigation (55.3 percent) and technical expertise (59.6 percent) where many of us spend our book hours.

It takes time to become a leader. If a young employee becomes impatient, then the boss will quickly identify that person as someone who is the antithesis of leadership and much less valuable to the team. According to the Addison Group, a provider of professional staffing services, and Kelton, a global insights firm, 40 percent of millennials expect a promotion every one to two years. So if leadership takes time to evaluate, young employees may be too impatient to reap the rewards (compensation and promotion).

In summary, here is the chasm:

- Employers want leadership.
- Employers will pay leaders more.
- Leadership takes time to evaluate.
- Young employees want more pay.
- Generally, young employees are not willing to wait.

This is not a societal problem for me to solve. Rather, this is a *huge opportunity* for a few young employees to leapfrog over their peers financially. If a young employee is patiently focused on developing leadership skills that translate to value for their employer, they will, in turn, experience the reward that impatience doesn't enjoy.

I know you can stand out and make the money you desire. It just takes a little effort and time. Now, when you make money, I want to make sure you don't lose it all. That's what happens to some people when they get a divorce. Let's talk a little about this in the next chapter.

Age 25: The Money Side Of Marriage

"Most people will never become wealthy in one generation if they are married to people who are wasteful."

—Thomas J. Stanley, *author*

Most research suggests that our brain hasn't fully developed until age twenty-five. This is good, but we are still subject to money mistakes. For that reason, I suggest you take a quick detour and read age seventy-nine and implement some of strategies discussed in that particular chapter.

Twenty-two percent of all divorce is a result of problems with money. It sounds overly simplistic, doesn't it? With the complexity of relationships isn't there something deeper such as irreconcilable differences, poor communication, substance abuse, or anger management challenges?

Grey's Anatomy and the political rhetoric from a bunch of overambitious divorced politicians have cast doubt on the importance of marriage. Don't be fooled. Marriage has many relational and societal benefits.

Let me give you another reason to fight for marriage—a financial one. If you get a divorce, it is highly likely that the female will be impoverished. Poverty may not hit her today, but it is likely to hit her in her sixties or seventies. The reality is that not many employers care to hire older female workers whose skill sets might not translate into the modern-day workforce. This is not right, but it is a reality and it subjects many women to a life of financial hardship.

Of course, when a young wife is divorced and must care for the children the pressure is exponentially exhausting. In fact, according to Healthy Marriage, 24 percent of divorced women with children are living in poverty. Compare that statistic to the 1 percent of married women with children who are living with poverty.

If you are about to get married, get on the same page before tying the knot. Premarital counseling results in 31 percent less likelihood of divorce. Don't get married without premarital counseling. If you can work with a local church or family counselor to open discussions about money behavior, you will improve your chances of marital success.

Divorce has serious financial consequences.

I recently had to separate a $500,000 investment account between a couple in their seventies getting a divorce. Both felt they lost the financial negotiations. They both did lose. When the couple has separate cell phone plans and separate grocery bills, $250,000 will not last as long. A different home and new utilities will eat away the bucket of money split in two. Financial life just got a little more difficult for this couple.

I love seeing old couples holding hands. That will be you! With that said, a home purchase may be a part of your evening conversations. If so, you'll need to put reasonable boundaries on the purchase so it's not just an emotional buy. I'll show you how to do this in the next chapter.

Age 26: A More Realistic Home Purchase

"Here lies Walter Fielding. He bought a house, and it killed him."

— Walter Fielding, *The Money Pit*

Homeownership is beautiful, but it does come at a price. It costs a lot to pay the mortgage, fix the air conditioning, and repair the holes in the walls. That's why the decision to buy shouldn't be taken lightly. For many people, renting is perfectly A-OK.

If you are like I was when I bought my first home, you don't have the 20 percent down payment needed to be a homeowner. That's a lot of money to come up with. There is hope, but not without sacrifice. Below are rules for the next generation who are planning their first home purchase.

Rule #1: Set a Firm Mortgage Budget

Calculate your combined household income. Then, multiply 25 percent of your take-home pay (after health insurance, taxes, etc.). This is the maximum amount you can spend on a fifteen-year mortgage payment, including property taxes and insurance.

Rule #2: Reassess Your Target with Humility

Stick to your budget and appreciate what you have in this season of life. You won't get a home that compares to the one your parents are living in now. It took them years and years of hard work to get where they are. Be patient. It will take time for you as well. Today, there is a hunger that gobbles up delayed gratification. Don't fall for this mortgage money trap called impatience.

Here's how to reassess your target home price relative to the marketplace.

In 2017, the average home price in the United States was $200,000 according to www.realtor.org. The median age in the US is thirty-six. Therefore, set your standard accordingly. For example, if you are twenty-five, then take your age and divide it by the average: 25/36 = 69.4 percent.

Then multiply 69.4 percent times the average home price: 0.694 X $200,000 = $138,888. This amount should put reality and perspective to your homeownership plan.

Keep in mind that regardless of the price you uncovered, you still can't violate Rule #1.

Rule #3: Save Windfalls

The goal is to save for the 20 percent down payment on the home. Saving windfalls is the most effective way to fast-forward a home purchase. All tax refunds, gifts, and proceeds from odd jobs and garage sales should go toward the home fund.

Drive Uber, sell junk, deliver pizzas, and do whatever it takes for extra cash. Swallow your pride for a season . . . it won't last forever.

You can't just lay out a plan for home ownership and expect it to be perfect. However, if you set out a plan, you increase the probability of success. Follow the above rules and you will be a part of the one of the greatest wealth-building tools in our country—home ownership.

Whether, you own a house or rent an apartment, you have a home. A home is full of life and memories. Because our life has value we need to protect it. This means it's that time to get insurance. Next, I'll tell you which ones to get right away.

Age 27: Insuring The Goose That Lays The Golden Eggs

"Whatever excuses you may have for not buying life insurance now will only sound ridiculous to your widow."

—Unknown

Pretty Woman star, Julia Roberts, bought insurance to cover her smile in the amount of $3 million. Las Vegas star Tom Jones had his chest hair insured for $7 million. You can get insurance for just about anything, including if your fiancé gets cold feet. Yes, there is wedding insurance. Although unique insurance policies are interesting and entertaining, most insurance is simply dry. Despite the disinterest, you must own the following four types of insurance:

1. ***Life Insurance:*** Our team at PAX Financial Group usually recommends our clients to purchase ten times their income in life insurance to protect those who depend on that income and to pay off debts. Stay-at-home spouses should own one half of the working spouse's coverage. I work with one widow who is employed only because she wants to. She shows up every day knowing she can quit because her husband left her enough money to live without forced employment. This is freedom and peace.

2. ***Disability Insurance:*** Buy 60 percent of your gross income in *long-term* disability insurance with a ninety-day waiting period. First buy through your employer and then shop the open markets with an individual plan. This is not an insurance to ignore; the leading causes of disability are not just falling off ladders. Rather they are musculoskeletal/

connective tissue disorders such as neck and back pain (28.5 percent), cancer (14.6 percent), injuries (10.6 percent), and mental disorders (8.9 percent). We filed a claim while my business partner was disabled. The money was vital to keep us going.

3. ***Health Insurance:*** It's tempting to avoid purchasing health insurance. But, cancer and car accidents know no age and the financial impact could burden you for life. When shopping, like most purchases, buy the best plan with the cheapest cost. But, have a dialogue with the agent to make sure your doctors and medicines are covered adequately.

4. ***Identity Theft Insurance:*** If you frequently make purchases on the internet using debit cards, you will likely get hacked one day. Not only will you have money stolen, you will have to take time and energy to get your financial life back in order. The mean total out-of-pocket loss for those victimized with identity theft in 2014 was $2,895. Most coverages like IDShield and Lifelock offer fraud monitoring and alerts at similar prices. Check out independent third-party reviews to identify the unique differences that might be better for your situation.

You will never have probabilities in your favor when evaluating insurance. In other words, there will never be an insurance company so stupid to insure something that has a 90 percent chance of paying a claim. With every insurance you buy, you are buying against the odds. Accept this fact. However, you are protecting yourself and your family should you be the unlucky one to fall victim.

Outside of the above four referenced insurance policies, most other coverage types will be personal decisions. You will need to ask yourself two questions: (a) What are the chances, based on my background and experience, that I might get financially banged up, and (b) can I afford to cover the event if it gets too expensive? For example, if you have a history of cancer in your family, you may consider cancer insurance even though most of your health insurance will take care of you. Or, if you have a concern about lawsuits, the purchase of an umbrella policy could make sense.

In summary, insure your life and your identity as if you are protecting the goose. Then, make practical decisions about protecting the house, car, and other golden eggs.

It may seem like a drain on your money, but insurance is needed. Children may seem like a financial drain as well. I'll share with you the cost in the next section. It's scary, but hasn't stopped me from having four beautiful children.

Age 28: The Cost Of Kids

"The formula for achieving middle-class success is simple: Finish high school; don't have a child before the age of 20; and get married before having the child."

— Larry Elder, American radio commentator

It ain't cheap to raise children. Per a study conducted by the USDA in 2013, parents spend around $13,000 per year per child. Love supersedes selfishness, and individuals forgo the new car and the vacation for the privilege of raising a child.

Now, for most people the extra cost is housing. The arrival of children raises an awareness for the need of a little elbow room. Add the increased expenses of health care and food with housing costs and you've accounted for most of the cost of child rearing.

If you decide to have three or four children, you get something we business people call "economies of scale." This is the idea that costs don't continue to go up at the same pace because resources are shared. Bunk beds, bulk cereal, and discounts on family health insurance prevent the third child from costing another $13,000 annually. The research from USDA states that parents spend around 22 percent less per child when adding a third or fourth child.

Overall, the lifetime expense for raising a child is close to $250,000. I have four children. In other words, I have $1 million of investments. To me it's an investment, not a liability or cost. With that attitude, I don't get discouraged because I don't compare my pile of toys to my peers'. I adjust my lifestyle to account for the cost of raising children.

My point in this section is this: don't be discouraged as money gets tighter with each child. They are a blessing. Somehow, despite the financial costs, we all find a way to make money life with children work.

I waited to introduce you to budgeting after you have children. Usually, that's when I can get a person's attention. In the next section, I'll provide a couple of budgeting options that minimize the risk of having to move back in with your parents.

Age 29: Budgeting For Those Not Good At Budgeting

"How did you go bankrupt? Two ways. Gradually, then suddenly."

— Ernest Hemingway, *American novelist*

Most people who are winning with money know how much is going toward food, shelter, and clothing. If I quizzed you on the spot, could you tell me what you spend?

Don't feel bad, most people can't spew out household budget numbers off the top of their head. But it is time to get familiar with your numbers more regularly.

Here is a starter approach to slicing up your budget. The rule is called the 50/30/20 Rule (this is a slight variation from Harvard bankruptcy expert Elizabeth Warren's rule used in her book *All Your Worth: The Ultimate Lifetime Money Plan.*) In this starter approach you should carve out 50 percent of your spending for needs, 20 percent should go toward paying down debt and/or saving, and 30 percent should go toward wants.

Does this approach make sense? Yes.

Let's start with why I like the 20 percent part. The reason I like this rule is because I find it to be consistent when working with those who are about to retire. Many people about to PIVOT (retire) find themselves needing around 80 percent of their preretirement income. This is not an overnight fix. It happens when you pay down consumer debt and stop funding Roth IRAs. Then, a chunk of the 20 percent in the 50/30/20 budget goes away.

The reason I like the 30 percent part is because it gives you freedom to enjoy life, have fun, and blow money. According to a Gallup poll, two-thirds of all Americans don't stick to a budget. This means that two-thirds of all Americans have no cap on blowing money and eating out. "Fun" money restraint is only a feeling not a discipline for most Americans. It's important for you to know that if you are in debt, lowering your wants to 20 percent or 10 percent will get you out from under your pile of debt much faster. It just takes a season of having less of what you "want."

To go a little deeper with our blow money here, it is critical to respect the subconscious influence marketing has on our decision-making. Marketers will use clever psychological tools called anchoring, repetition, and priming effects to influence our decision-making. And when we buy, we say, "Thank you . . . for tricking me."

For example, let's say that that a retail store wants to sell you a Kenneth Cole jacket for $195. At first glance, it may be expensive. However, if they put a similar Ralph Lauren Polo next to it for $225, they know you'll grab the Kenneth Cole, thinking you got a good deal. This is one of hundreds of tricks retailers use to influence the way you purchase.

To minimize the risk of this retail influence and marketing overload, put a firm cap on wants. It can be a cap on all wants or just areas that need self-control, like dining, vacations, clothes, or enter-tainment.

The 50 percent of spending on needs is a critical boundary should life take a turn. If you have a major health issue, become disabled, become unemployed, or are forced into early retirement, then this 50 percent number is your most important number. Knowing what it takes each month just to survive is critical because of life's uncertainties.

With that said, this rule of thumb does fall short. The 50/30/20 rule reminds me of many different weight-loss strategies. Weight-loss and budget strategies are only as good as your discipline and focus.

The 50/30/20 rule will stabilize your weight but you'll never be healthy, vibrant, and optimistic. That's why I would recommend that you start with the 50/30/20 rule but quickly graduate to a more effective strategy called baby steps through Financial Peace University (FPU). This program, developed by nationally syndicated talk show host Dave Ramsey, helps you and your family work together to develop money disciplines.

I did the Financial Peace University in my late twenties. My wife and I went down to one car, and we, along with our newborn, lived like minimalists. It didn't last long and wasn't too painful (in retrospect). FPU helped pull us out of the hole. It's one of the best investments of our family time.

Done in a Decade(ish)
1. Set up an online money-tracking system
2. Paid cash for a car
3. Set aside a minimum three-month emergency fund
4. Set up a consistent (monthly) charitable giving plan
5. Started saving an automatic 15%
6. Developed leadership skills to maximize employment opportunities
7. Received pre-marital counseling
8. Obtained a 15 year Mortgage with 20% down
9. Purchased the four types of insurance coverage
10. Established a budget
11. Attended Financial Peace University

Age 30: The Best Wealth Way . . . A 401(K)

"Why didn't you sign up for your company's 401k?"
"I'd never be able to run that far."

— Dilbert

In 2008, we experienced the Great Recession. Many investors who had exposure to the stock market saw the value of their 401(k)s drop dramatically. The running joke in the midst of tears was that a 401(k) was now a 201(k). Then, the skeptics, critics, and opportunists seized the opportunity to discourage Americans from investing in their 401(k) plan.

Don't be discouraged . . .

The 401(k) is one of the best ways to accumulate wealth.

Our team at PAX Financial Group encourages our clients to contribute the most possible in a 401(k), depending on the person's debt load.

A 401(k) is a section of the tax code that allows employers to take money from your check and put it in an investment account. This money reduces your taxable income creating an immediate benefit for you. Then, many employers will match a portion of what you put in.

Remember, you aren't actually investing in a 401(k), you are investing what is inside of it.

Here's another cool thing about 401(k)s not many people talk about—for long-term investors, historical returns have generally been positive. For the eighty-nine-year period between 1825 and 2013, the stock market was up 71 percent of the time.

However, when you catch a negative year (the other 29 percent) and you are putting money in each month, you are buying shares on sale!

Finally, the sweetest spot of a 401(k)—employer contributions! It is free money and simply foolish if you don't get it.

The idea of your money compounding more rapidly due to the tax deferral in a 401(k) is a powerful long-term tool. For some people, the other powerful way to grow your wealth is by starting a business. As a longtime entrepreneur, I have some critical thoughts for you to consider before you make that leap. I'll share those thoughts in the next chapter.

Age 31: Before You Start Your Business

"The best investment is an undiversified investment, when you are right."

— Unknown

Today, it is so easy to start a business. You can offer your outdated clothing on Craiglist.com. You can sell your design skills on Fiverr.com. You can even raise capital for your next idea on Gofundme.com if you can't get an appearance on *Shark Tank*.

This entrepreneur dream is embedded in my heart. I started a business, my parents started a business, my brother is an entrepreneur, and so is my sister. Our entire family is passionate about the entrepreneurial dream. If being a small business owner is calling you, then grab your belief, sprinkle it with money, and fuel it with hard work. That's what it takes to start a business. Even though the startup business is not certain and completely undiversified, you still place the bet because the bet is on . . . you.

It's a game of risk versus reward and you must be smart about nudging the odds in your favor of success.

Generally speaking, the odds are against you at the starting gate. According to Bloomberg, there is an 80 percent chance that you will fail within the first eighteen months. Many fail because they haven't set reasonable expectations about the trials and/or they mismanage their money. However, when you set up your business the right way from the beginning, your preparations will move probabilities in your favor.

When you commit to starting a business, it is important that you establish the following to maintain a sense of financial order.

First, you should have six months of personal expenses set aside for an emergency fund prior to launching. Protecting your mortgage with cash in the bank will take some pressure off the startup business. This is called your runway.

Then, take your Employer Identification Number (EIN) and assumed name certificate to the local bank and open a separate bank account from your personal account. Also, open a business savings account and transfer 25 percent of your business net income into the savings account for income taxes. This is an estimated percentage, but one that will get you starting a healthy habit before your CPA gives you a specific number.

Finally (and most importantly) ask a group of at least three business owners to be your advisory council. Don't demand much; just ask that they be open to help you grow your business. Shoot them group emails when you get stuck or discouraged. As fellow entrepreneurs, they may be the only voices that push you through tough times.

You're ready to take the small-business plunge! Now, you may be hit with the reality that some months, cash flow is tight. Regardless of cash flow volatility you must find a way to start saving for this upcoming financial obligation. If you don't save early, you could devastate your PIVOT plan.

Age 32: Saving for Your Kid's College

"The best way to avoid a debt crisis in college is to start saving early."

— Unknown

Soccer Mom and Football Dad, don't fight the odds. According to College Solution, the average NCAA athletic scholarship is less than $11,000. Think about this: your collective spending on private lessons and expensive gear will result in a return on investment of $11,000. Any good businessperson will tell you that it's not a good deal.

Maybe your child is uniquely talented and can hit the baseball farther or has mastered a back handspring before all her friends. In this case, you just might fall into the category of getting blessed with an athletic scholarship. If you believe it's sustainable both physically and emotionally, you're not being realistic. Only 2 percent of high school seniors actually get a sports scholarship.

Part of your concern that motivates your athletic investments may be the idea of the looming higher-education bill. Yes, the cost of higher education is out of control. According to the College Board, a "moderate" college budget will be around $25,000 per year for an in-state public college. With most families simply fighting to keep health costs down, a $100,000 bill is beyond frightening. No wonder we parents put so much pressure on athletic excellence!

Below are a few ways to alleviate the pain.

1. Start saving early. Should you be fortunate enough to start saving the day you receive your child's Social Security

number, it would require you to set aside $150 per month to pay for a four-year state tuition (assuming a 10 percent annual rate of return). However, each year you wait, you'll need to add to that $150 outlay. Don't delay, start saving now no matter how late you are.

2. Consider a non-traditional approach. Too many students spend $100,000 on a degree that has zero relevance and application to employers. As an alternative, your child may be an incredible dental hygienist whose profession just so happens to have a median pay of $72,330 per year. Or maybe they can deploy their video game skills in a peripheral skill like a web developer whose median pay is $64,970 per year.

3. Think outside the big name universities. Some accredited four-year universities have lower costs than the ones with brick and mortar and expensive faculty. By working with the local community they are able to create relevant four-year degrees at a fraction of the price.

The above three ideas are just scratching the surface of the many ways to absorb the cost of higher education. Start thinking now about how to be creative and unique so your neglect doesn't bankrupt your family.

You will find it refreshing to have a college savings plan. But, while college is difficult enough with parents, it is even more challenging without them. As a mom and dad, make sure you think about what life might be like if you passed away. This next conversation will be uncomfortable but possibly one of the most important chapters you will read.

Age 33: The Guardian Of Your Children

"It's always harder to be the one left behind than the one who leaves."

— Tamara Ecclestone, British model

I often ask my clients about their postmortem plans by beginning with the phrase, "Should you have passed away last night by a meteor hitting your home, what would happen to . . ." The question is set up as "last night" and "meteor" to avoid the subconscious thought of "jinxing" an outcome.

Regardless of how it's postured, we have to talk about life and death.

One of the most important proclamations that must be written down by parents is who becomes guardian if the parents pass away. The last thing you want is for the courts to hand your kids over to crazy family members. Don't depend on strangers to decide who takes care of your children when you die. Identify the guardian now.

Below are four considerations when establishing your guardian . . .

1. **Complete your will.** Most people have either

    (a) thought about but not executed;

    (b) executed but not signed; or

    (c) actually fully executed a will.

    Set the roadblocks aside and complete the will for the purpose of writing down exactly who you want to take care of the kids. The establishment of a guardian is processed in conjunction with a will.

2. **Name someone who shares the same values.** Do you want your child to attend church? Is it your desire to have your child carry the same passion for humanity that you have right now? If so, make sure your guardian will honor your heart and continue to instill those same values after you pass away.

3. **Separate the money from the kids.** You should assign someone to take care of the money and someone else to raise the kids. In fact, the best family to take care of the kids may not be the best financial people. You can pick a trustee at a financial institution or a friend who can help pay bills for your children but it doesn't have to be the guardian.

4. **Get life insurance.** Make sure your guardian knows they are responsible for feeding new mouths *and* that you have acquired enough life insurance to provide for this.

The only time someone brings up the topic of life and death before I do is if a tragic event made national news. This decision-making is not rooted in logic and is called "recency bias" by behavioral finance people. This means that we, generally, aren't willing to plan for our family, until death disturbs us.

- If it's a death in Ethiopia, it's concerning.
- If it's in Europe, it's sad.
- If it's in America, it hurts.
- If it's in your state, it's tragic.
- If it's in your city, it's scary.
- If it's in your neighborhood, it's tearful.
- If it's you, it's too late.

I don't want to put a guilt trip on you but if you love your children you will take the little time, money, and effort to ensure they are well taken care of should something happen to mom and dad. Now, on a more positive note, your financial future and your PIVOT might work extremely well if you own the type of investment we discuss in the next chapter.

Age 34: Investing In Real Estate

"Don't wait to buy real estate. Buy real estate and wait."

— Will Rogers, actor

Don't get in the real estate business unless you have a passion for it. However, if you have the passion and can exchange the touchy feely side for tough business acumen, then real estate could be for you.

There are two major categories of real estate: commercial and residential. According to Investopedia, the average rate of return for the past twenty years (ending June 2015) on commercial real estate was 9.5 percent. Alternatively, residential real estate outperformed its counterpart with an average annual return of 10.6 percent. Both of those historical returns will be more than sufficient to help you meet your goals of retiring and beating inflation.

However, when we look at the word "average" in the phrase "average rate of return," you must consider that some real estate owners were winners and some were losers.

You lose by getting caught up in the emotional side of owning real estate with lack of preparation. You win by making an unemotional, objective purchase factoring the value of . . . yield.

If real estate is a cow, yield is the milk . . . not the beef. Residential real estate investors call this "net rental income." Commercial real estate investors call yield "cap rates."

A target yield changes frequently. Some years, real estate yield is higher than others. It has a backward type of behavior: yield goes down when real estate prices are hot, and goes up when times are scary and credit is scarce.

But how is it calculated?

Suppose we buy a cute little two-bedroom house in the suburbs for $100,000 cash. The home is pretty close to the university so we strategize to rent to a few students in the hopes they don't trash it. We place an ad and five minutes later, the home is rented. Now, we own the home but still need to pay taxes, insurance, and repair broken pipes. Each month we collect rent, pay the bills, and pocket the rest. After we fix the final roof leak at the end of the last semester, we realize we made $9,600 in net income. The yield is 9.6 percent ($9,600/$100,000).

The yield sounds pretty good right? Maybe. What if the year is 1980 and putting the money into a bank account would yield a 12 percent return without the hassle of toilet repairs or a frat party?

If our commercial or residential real estate only provides a yield of 3 percent, we will need to be honest with ourselves. What if we could sell the 3 percent property and park the money in a hassle-free 5 percent investment? If we don't pay attention to yield, we are just betting that the property will increase in value over time. Smart long-term real estate investors don't rely solely on hopeful real estate appreciation; they want yield too.

Real estate is an attractive long-term investment but will never be attainable for those people who get sucked into making decisions that are a reaction to what their friends are buying. This adult type of peer pressure is our next conversation.

Age 35: Adult Peer Pressure

"The happy man is the one that earns $100 more than his wife's brother."

— Unknown

According to Jonah Berger, the author of *Contagious*, it is suggested that one in ten Americans tell the other nine how to vote, where to eat, and what to buy. Of course, if you are like me, you're thinking . . . not me . . . I think for myself. But let's not be so confident, our friends (on and off Facebook) do influence our thinking.

It's time to acknowledge that the people around us influence our subconscious wallet. Then, without knowing, at the end of the month/year we are left wondering where all our money went.

There are seven purchases that are influenced by our peers.

1. Vehicles. I know our identity is tied to the car we drive. But, we must get comfortable with what we can afford regardless of our friend's ride. Let someone else struggle to make a $700 monthly car payment. Life will catch up and they'll regret the purchase.

2. Children's Education. There is debate with private school, public school, and homeschool. I'm agnostic in this space because I see authentic merits for all three. However, don't get trapped in the fact that because all your friends are moving one direction with education, that you are the neighborhood fool. Stand firm on what you can afford.

3. Technology. Getting the latest gadgets is like an addiction. If you waited five months for the Nintendo 3DS you would have saved eighty dollars. Be patient with technology; it's much easier than trying to keep up.

4. Drinking Habits. According to the Bureau of Labor Statistics, the average American spends about 1 percent of their income on alcohol. Even if you aren't drinking more, your drinking bill is still going up each year as the price and taxes associated with this market continue to rise with the demand. Be cautious and develop habits of self-control.

5. Social Club Memberships. Gym memberships and country clubs can be costly. It's not only the monthly bill, but the ancillary costs such as dining and social functions. If you aren't prepared financially to afford the social influence of these organizations, wait before you join.

6. Home. Your home mortgage should be no more than 25 percent of your take-home pay. Yet, many people quickly get caught in the dream because they see new home buys on Instagram. What you may not know is that your buddy with the nice house made the down payment with money inherited from his late grandma. Don't try to keep up. Stick with your own personal budget.

7. Vacations. It is hard not to covet the Cabo San Lucas Facebook posts. Don't get sucked in. Memories can be made with weekend road trips and a picnic blanket. In fact, that's the way most of us in the middle class do it anyway. And it doesn't require an American Express card.

It takes maturity and awareness to prevent the influence of peers from robbing our wallet. Let's be the hero of our family by not becoming a conforming spender.

Never be discouraged

No one is exactly where they want to be financially. No one. Sure, you have made mistakes. But that's because you are human.

Regardless of your age, make the small money changes today and compounded over time you will see improvement.

It starts today.

Age 36: Eating Wealth

"Your net worth to the world is usually determined by what remains after your bad habits are subtracted from your good ones."

— Benjamin Franklin, Founding Father of the United States of America

According to the United States Department of Agriculture, the average monthly cost to feed a family of four "at home" on a moderate budget is $883.10 per month. At-home dinner table eating is not cheap by itself. But when it's mixed with irresponsible restaurant dining, life can get out of control quickly.

As you can tell by the parking lots, dining out is America's new favorite pastime—leapfrogging baseball. In fact, if a family spends $883.10 per month on groceries they'll usually spend another $500 dining out each month.

Unfortunately, dining out is eating most of our paycheck. Generally, restaurants mark up items 300 percent in addition to the tips, travel, sales tax, alcohol, and sweet teas. It is critical that you put a dollar cap on the convenience of dining out. It is becoming the thief of financial progress.

It's difficult for me to tell you where your family needs to go to find the sweet spot of food spending. Various family sizes, diets, and even regional information make it challenging to give you a firm spending number. The number is somewhere between ramen noodles and Morton's Steakhouse.

If you can't find the cash to give and save, you must stop eating out! The money is likely in your belly.

As a financial advisor, I have difficult conversations with people who say, "I just don't have the cash to pay down debt, save, or give." The reason it's uncomfortable is because I know that the money is at Chili's. When you go to a financial advisor, you may or may not have that uncomfortable conversation. The framework is up to you. The topic of this professional relationship is the focus of our next chapter.

Age 37: Hiring An Advisor

"It's funny how I'm good at giving advice to others, but when it comes to helping myself, I don't know what to do."

— hplyrikz.com

There are five situations when you should hire a financial advisor.

1. You have paid off consumer debt.
In this scenario, after all credit cards and car loans are paid, you should have enough monthly cash flow to start a Roth IRA. Not all investment firms will accept a starter account. So, check around and ask if they accept zero-dollar minimums.

2. You need to simplify your investments.
You have old 401(k)s and little IRAs that have their faces on a milk carton. You can't even recall amounts and investment selections. It is important to organize your investments in such a way that you can know if they are working or if they are broken. A financial advisor will help you with this.

3. You are making emotional investment decisions.
If you are honest with yourself, you realize that you aren't that good at managing your Charles Schwab trading account. Although you have a few wins, collectively your returns aren't flattering. When you are honest about your results, you'll realize how quickly emotions and gut feelings interfere with results. An advisor will help you make decisions using reason based on evidence rather than emotions.

4. You are five years away from PIVOTing (retirement).

Preparations and adjustments must be made prior to PIVOTing. For example, should you buy life insurance or get a survivor benefit plan? Or, what decisions do you need to make about health insurance? Also, there are budget conversations that must happen before the income adjusts. Don't wait until the last day to engage an experienced professional to have these talks.

5. You are too busy.

You are perfectly capable both emotionally and intellectually handling your money. But, you don't have time. You are focused on work, family, and life and you've neglected the details.

*Visit the **Age 67** chapter for more information about finding a financial advisor.*

Although there isn't a standard dollar amount in the industry, there are still competent advisors without a minimum dollar requirement. PAX Financial Group has taken the opposite approach of the industry and is committed to not having a minimum required starting investment amount.

The key is to evaluate the competency of the advisor and confirm the level of service and attention. Long-term, the relationship with the right advisory team could be one of the most important relationships in your life.

There will be around a 1 to 2 percent additional cost to your investment assets to hire an advisor. But, according to a 2016 research study by Vanguard titled "Putting Value on Your Value: Quantifying Vanguard Advisor's Alpha," a financial advisor (under certain circumstances) can provide as much as 3 percent in *additional* annual net returns.

However, the potential 3 percent benefit is small potatoes compared to the real money threat. A 25 percent mistake on your money will leave you wishing you would have not been so frugal in this one area of life. Day in and day out, hairstylists fix bad haircuts. But unlike bad haircuts, bad investing has lots of zeros on them. Let's not get a bad haircut in this next important investment strategy.

Age 38: Senator Roth IRA

"Yes, America is in a new era of opportunity. Some have called it the Reagan era, I could as easily call it the Roth era..."

— Remarks at a 1988 fund-raising speech for former Senator William V. Roth

A Roth IRA (named after Senator Roth from Delaware) allows you to make contributions annually and the monies grow tax-free if used for retirement. If you follow the rules, you will not pay any taxes when you take money out at retirement. This tax-free benefit is the reason most Americans should be investing in a Roth IRA.

I love the idea of foregoing the immediate tax deduction from the good ol' traditional IRA to get future tax-free retirement income. Plus, there are other huge benefits you get from a Roth at retirement such as (a) no required minimum distributions; (b) possibly lower medical costs because of lower retirement taxable income; (c) protection from a raise in tax rates; and (d) no taxes on social security from Roth IRA distributions.

The one exception to the Roth IRA is Mr. Frugal High Tax Bracket. This is someone who has a high income but lives way below his means.

If you are in a high tax bracket and haven't had lifestyle creep, you may want the immediate deduction.

For the Mr. Frugal High Tax Bracket take the tax deduction of 35 percent today and deal with the 25 percent taxable income later.

Outside of Mr. Frugal High Tax Bracket, the team at PAX Financial

Group believes everyone should consider a Roth IRA.

The above ideas apply to the Roth 401(k) as well.

Finally, remember that you never invest in a Roth IRA, you invest in what is inside, and the Roth is the way the IRS knows how to tax it— or not.

If you don't have enough cash flow to invest in a Roth IRA, you will need to get a bigger shovel (i.e., a new job). I have conversations with thirty-year-olds every week about frustrating careers. You are not alone. But if you want to get better, it requires you to think a little differently and address the critical career questions that must be answered.

Age 39: Dead-End Job

"The only way to do great work is to love what you do. If you haven't found it yet, keep looking. Don't settle."

— Steve Jobs, American entrepreneur and business magnate

According to a Gallup poll, 70 percent of people either hate their jobs or are completely disengaged. Do you have a dead-end job?

If you are one of the 70 percent, don't stay there. Not only is it demoralizing, your apathy will discourage your boss to give you a raise or promotion.

Reframe your dead-end career path by listening to Greg McKeown, the author of *Essentialism*, as he suggests you should spend time developing answers to these three questions . . .

1. What do I feel deeply inspired by?

2. What am I particularly talented at?

3. What can I do to help with a significant need in the world?

I would add another question to Greg's three:

4. How do I make money all the while answering the first three questions?

If your answers to those questions do not line up with your vocation, it's time for a switch. You have much more to offer this world than a rat in a race. You just need to find your meaning before you shift career paths.

Internationally renowned psychiatrist Victor E. Frankl endured the terror and horror of Nazi death camps. His insights were well-documented in his book, *Man's Search for Meaning*. In his experience and research he recognized "When the impossibility of replacing a person is realized, it allows the responsibility which a man has for existence and continuance to appear in all its magnitude." Read this again.

Have you felt that you have yet to be introduced to the world in "all of your magnitude?" At age thirty-nine, about to turn forty, it's time to set aside your previous approach to your job and re-introduce yourself to the world. You can do this!

Done in a Decade
1. Contributed to 401(k)
2. Considered starting a business
3. Used a 529 plan to save for college
4. Established legal documents including guardian
5. Bought real estate
6. Identified the spending habits of the five people closest to you
7. Set a dining out budget
8. Hired a financial advisor
9. Set up a Roth IRA
10. Evaluated your career path

Age 40: Mutual Funds And Exchange-Traded Funds*

"How many millionaires do you know who have become wealthy by investing in savings accounts? I rest my case."

— Robert G. Allen, American motivational speaker

Y ou likely share a last name with your uncle's son. You have commonalities but, yet, are different. Notice that "mutual" and "exchange-traded" share the same last name ("funds") as well. Their commonality exists in the fact that they both own a wide number of stocks or bonds so that no individual loser investment causes the entire investment plan to crash. Their similarity is in their diversification and they both can work well.

They have a handful of differences (tax efficiency, intraday trading, etc.), though. The main difference is in how they buy their stocks and bonds. Mutual funds use people known as fund managers to select the stocks and bonds. But exchange-traded funds (ETFs) (typically focused on index investing) use sophisticated computers, formulas, and algorithms to select the stocks and bonds, and only make major "tweaks" periodically.

Because ETFs avoid fund managers and active trading, their costs are considerably different. ETFs are, generally, much less expensive. In 2016, this fee difference contributed to the S&P 500 Index (often purchased through ETFs) outperforming 88.30 percent of all large-cap mutual funds. That's quite a difference. Why even bother with mutual funds if they get beat up by their cousins?

However, some mutual funds have indeed outperformed their index over time using systems, processes, and good people and . . . they aren't that hard to find. You just have to look a little.

What should you own? Start your strategy with the low-cost-index ETFs and then identify mutual funds that have outperformed their index over five or ten years. Yes, there is debate in this area of finance, but it is intellectually dishonest to completely discount the beautiful and effective combination of passive-index ETFs and active mutual funds. They both work well and both will help you accumulate wealth.

With all that said, I would suggest to you that we have the wrong argument. Frankly, it doesn't materially matter if you decide to own active mutual funds or if you decide to lower your cost through ETFs. Both funds are simply the ingredients. If you want to pay attention to your investments, spend less time with the ingredients and focus on the recipe (next chapter).

Mutual Funds and Exchange Traded Funds (ETF's) are sold by prospectus. Please consider the investment objectives, risks, charges, and expenses carefully before investing. The prospectus, which contains this and other information about the investment company, can be obtained from the Fund Company or your financial professional. Be sure to read the prospectus carefully before deciding whether to invest.

Age 41: The Investment Recipe

"The stock market is a device to transfer money from the impatient to the patient."

— Warren Buffett, American business magnate and investor

Knowing that the majority of the time the ingredients will be some combination of mutual funds and ETFs, how do we construct the recipe? This is an important question, because, frankly, middle-class investors have historically been poor cooks, costing their families hundreds of thousands of dollars over time. Consider this: the average rate of return for the stock market from 1996 to 2016 was 7.68 percent. The average investor return was 4.79 percent.

Dalbar has published this study every April and ending in 2016, it had been twenty-three years. In every single year, for twenty-three straight years, the stock market has outperformed investors.

At the expense of overusing the "cooking" theme, below is the recipe to increase the odds that your investment meal doesn't burn.

WARNING: GETTING TECHNICAL

First, for long-term investors, you should add spice. To check how aggressive you are, check your investment portfolio beta. Beta (usually) measures volatility relative to the stock market. If it is less than one, get it in the ballpark of around beta one. If you get it closer to one, you will be closer to the overall stock market's characteristics (returns, risk, etc.) Many people water down their recipe out of fear and take on too little risk (beta of 0.5). If you are diversified, don't fret about getting a beta of one...from 1825 to 2013, the market was up 71 percent of the time. The odds are in your favor when you add the additional risk to your portfolio.

Second, don't experiment with ingredients you don't understand. If you take on too much risk by betting on certain sectors (i.e., energy, technology, etc.) it will take a long time to recover if the sector gets beat up. For example, if you lose 50 percent of your $10,000 investment, it will take 100 percent to break even. This 100 percent rate of return isn't easy to collect. Maybe you have inside knowledge on a stock or sector. Let's assume that you place a "bet" and it works. This scenario can be even worse than losing the first time because it begets overconfidence. The stock market has a peculiar way of humbling overconfident investors.

Finally, (and maybe most importantly) be patient with the cooking. Most investors don't stick around for a full market cycle. It takes around five years (fifty-six months) for a market cycle to experience an up and a down. Some people bail when it goes up because they assume others are making more and they don't want to miss out.

Others sell when it goes down because emotions and headlines hijack their brains. Stick to the plan. Successful investors don't abandon the strategy without experiencing the results over a full market cycle.

The funny thing about investing is that even if you get the ingredients and the recipe right, you still don't know the temperature of the oven. In other words, unlike setting the oven at 350 degrees and getting some level of predictability, we don't know with the same certainty how the markets will behave. Embrace the uncertainty. Those that accept the investing unknowns typically get rewarded over time. Those that avoid uncertainty stare at a pile of uncooked dough (pun intended) and never beat inflation or accumulate wealth.

Emotional mistakes with investments rob your wealth and so can consumer debt. If you have followed my conversations so far, you should not be in credit card debt or any other consumer debt. But, life happens. In the next chapter, I'll help you get out of it.

Age 42: If You Woke Up With Consumer Debt

"Ten percent of the borrowers in the world use debt to get richer – ninety percent use debt to get poorer."

— Robert Kiyosaki, author

No one just wakes up one day with a pile of debt. Debt is damage that resulted from poor money maintenance.

TransUnion claims that the average credit card debt is $4,878. Experian says that the average car loan is $30,032. Then, if you add on $26,700 of student debt (according to the New York Fed), you have about $61,610 of money burden. It's financially expensive and mentally exhausting to be an average borrower in America today.

How do we get out of all this consumer debt?

The debt snowball is an excellent approach to destroying debt. I have seen it work many times. The snowball effect places behavior above math. In essence, you will focus the majority of your cash flow toward the smallest balance first, and then snowball that payment into the next smallest balance. As you experience these little wins, you will gain the momentum of hope to become completely debt free.

However, before you debt snowball, add these financial steps to your strategy.

Step 1: Become the negotiator. Identify every reoccurring monthly payment being drafted from your account and cancel or negotiate the amounts. You will be surprised what is negotiable if you threaten to cancel.

Step 2: Send windfalls directly to debt. Apply all tax refunds, pay raises, bonuses, and income from side jobs to the debt. Only if you're serious about the financial future can you avoid the temptation of not spending windfalls.

If you want peace with money, get angry at debt. Debt needs to be an enemy.

I've been down the road of drowning in debt. I made a commitment to fix it. I'm proud of my commitment and I'm pleased with the results. It took years of discipline to get out of the debt hole, but it was worth it.

It is easy to get back into debt when you buy something you can't afford because you can't wait any longer. This happens all the time with home remodels. I'll help you avoid this mistake so it doesn't mess up your plan to PIVOT.

Age 43: Remodeling Your Kitchen

"A man builds a fine home, and now he has a master, and a task for life; he is to furnish, watch, show it, and keep it in repair, the rest of his days."

— **Ralph Waldo Emerson, poet**

In 2002, a survey of American homeowners who remodeled their kitchens found that, on average, they had expected the job to cost around $18,000. But how much did they really pay for the work done? I'll tell you in a second.

Even though the online world offers all the tips and financial tricks to prepare us financially for a home remodel, the emotional tug of luxury and efficiency pulls at our purse strings.

There are difficult decisions to be made with a remodel and most of us aren't as experienced as our friends Chip and Joanna Gaines from *Fixer Upper.*

According to a 2014 research project by Remodeling.hw.net, there is not more than a 100 percent recoup on your money for any particular remodel. In other words, the idea of getting your money back on the remodel of your home is not factual but rather rooted in wishful hope. This means that remodeling for the sole purpose of getting the money back is a bad decision.

Nationally, the best remodel is a steel door/entry. This recoups 96.6 percent of the cost. If you want to make a significant remodel by adding an attic bedroom, you would recoup about 84.3 percent of the cost when you resold your home.

Most realtors would suggest a kitchen remodel is low-hanging fruit. A minor kitchen remodel costs on average $18,856 and recoups 82.7 percent of the money when the house is sold. Additionally, it's important to know that, according to Kiplinger August 2016, 90 percent of buyers want a home with exterior lighting. If you want to make an instant impact that only costs around $63 to $135 per fixture, consider making this investment rather than a total remodel.

I considered etching a San Antonio Spurs logo into my carved stone but was convinced otherwise. Avoid (when possible) custom remodels that will only cater to a limited group of people. "Projects geared toward the homeowner's particular tastes, like the addition of a home music studio, have the least positive effect on asking price," says Owen Gilman, president of ISoldMyHouse.com.

To answer my question above, on average, remodels end up costing $20,000 more than the original estimate!

Plan carefully and know that most renovators make a lot of money on additions to the plan. They know humans and they know there is money to be made by not being prepared.

If you're doing a remodel, pay cash and stick to the budget.

Maybe you have remodeled and are proud of your new windows and countertops. However, your kids are looking out the window to college or, may even have one foot out the door. If that is the case, then you need to start getting ready right away.

Age 44: Close To College Preparation

"An investment in knowledge pays the best interest."

— Benjamin Franklin, Founding Father of the United States of America

Today, a sixteenth birthday for your princess or young man might peer pressure you into an automobile purchase. I hope you show some restraint. There are two other priority financial maneuvers to consider...

First, pause your monthly savings into the college account. Then, take the monthly outlay and use the cash flow to find a college coach. Despite having resources in high school through college counselors, you have probability already realized that their plates are full. You need someone focused on your child's specific needs.

Sitting down, kneecap-to-kneecap, with someone who understands your situation and aligns it with their experience is the ultimate objective at this age. Think about it, you are about to make a $100,000 investment. It makes sense to spend some time with an expert to increase the probability of a good return on investment.

Second, reduce risk in your portfolio. I hope at this point you have been relatively aggressive with your college planning and that the majority of the investments have been in stocks. However, it's time to reduce risk.

Imagine we have another 2008 financial crisis and your child is about to go to college. You have saved $50,000 and are proud of your discipline and preparation. Then, the market crashes, and your $50,000 magically turns to $30,000.

Of course, you don't want to sell at the bottom and permanently capture the losses. This happened to some of my clients in the actual 2008/2009 markets. We had to take loans to pay for college while the monies recovered. I don't want that to happen to you.

Go ahead and reduce your stock exposure in your college account down to 50 percent. It's still reasonable to have some stocks given that your time horizon is staggered over the four years in college. But, by removing the other half of the stocks, you are less exposed to a major financial pullback.

Age 45: Checkup Time

"However beautiful the strategy, you should occasionally look at the results."

— Winston Churchill, Former British Prime Minister

People who are winning with money think about increasing their net worth more than a tax refund or winning the lottery. This way of thinking requires periodic financial checkups.

Annual checkups increase the probability of financial success.

When doing a financial checkup, what should we look at? Below are the five items to evaluate when executing your annual financial checkup.

1. **Net Worth.** Has your net worth grown since the last time you took a snapshot? Net worth is defined by assets minus liabilities. Over the past year, you should have grown your assets by saving and making good investments and/or reduced your liabilities by paying down debt. There should be a trend in a positive direction.

2. **Insurance Coverage.** Do you have the adequate amount of life insurance, health insurance, disability, and identity theft coverage? The amounts and types can change based on your income and obligations changing. Also, the insurance companies periodically change product types and actuarial tables, so you may be able to acquire new coverage types or reduce costs.

3. **Spending.** It isn't uncommon that as your income goes up, so do your expenses. Take a pulse and see if they are

getting out of control. Look at the last year of spending and place them into major categories such as food, housing, medical, dining, and entertainment (just to name a few). Take a look with your spouse and a professional and view the categories of spending relative to income. Identify if there is overspending and opportunities to apply a degree of restraint going forward.

4. **Professional Relationships.** In this season of life, do you have the right accountants, attorneys, insurance agents, and other professionals to guide you? Maybe your complexity has outgrown their competency. Or, maybe the professional's business model has evolved to where their team can no longer meet your needs

5. **Investment Performance.** Frankly, reviewing investments more than annually is an exercise in futility that only leads to anxiety. Be sure to check, however, at least annually that you are performing well relative to (a) your personal goals and expectations; (b) the risk you are taking; and (c) the overall markets. As always, don't knee-jerk your decision to make change. If you're disappointed, make a note and pay attention to see if the disappointments become a trend.

I know life is busy, but if you fail to get professional financial checkups every year, you are being irresponsible with your money. If partnering with the right financial advisor, the conversation can be enjoyable, insightful, and worth the effort.

By implementing a checkup regularly, you move from discouragement to hope. It just takes a little time. Hopefully, this regular maintenance helps you prevent tax issues. That's the topic of our next chapter. I'll also share with you the odds of getting audited.

Age 46: Taxes And Audits

"You must pay taxes. But there's no law that says you've got to leave a tip."

— Morgan Stanley ad

First, pay your taxes.

I'll never forget my first IRS confrontation. I pray that it will be my last. I had my first year of 1099 income as a young just-out-of-college entrepreneur. No withholding was taken from my paycheck.

Then, April 15 approached and I had a bill for $10,000 with zero cash in the bank. I was scared and concerned. I called the IRS (not recommended) and begged for help. I'll never forget the lady on the other end of the phone who advised me. She said, "Young man, you don't need to negotiate with us (also known as an offer and compromise), you just need to pay it off and never do this again." It was motherly advice and I appreciated it.

If you are self-employed, you need to pay your quarterly taxes and not be tempted to spend the IRS's money. The IRS has even made it easy so you can transfer the funds quickly through https://www.eftps.gov/eftps/.

Second, be aware of the audit.

Now, suppose you paid your taxes and are committed to sending the IRS their money on a consistent basis. How, then, do you minimize the probability of the dreadful audit? Unfortunately, if you make more money, the chances are a bit higher. For example, according to the IRS in 2016, the IRS audited less than 0.62 percent of those making less than $200,000, but 1.01 percent of those making between $200,000 and $499,999, and 2.06 percent of those making between $500,000 and $999,999. I don't suppose anyone would intentionally make less money just to avoid an IRS audit.

However, your lack of integrity could also lead to an audit. Some business owners will blur the lines of integrity when communicating to the IRS. Don't fudge the numbers. If you fail to be honest, the IRS has developed a system that identifies dishonest figures.

According to Donald Duncan, founder of Chicago-based DC3 Financial Counselors, "The agency (IRS) uses occupational codes to measure typical amounts of travel by profession, and a tax return showing 20 percent or more above the norm might get a second look." You may legitimately have an anomaly in a certain area of your personal or business return. If so, keep impeccable records to defend yourself.

Most Certified Public Accountants (CPAs) and/or tax professionals know the rules. It is worth the expense to pay someone "in the know" to reduce the chance of an audit.

But who really likes to talk about the IRS, much less pay them? Most people enjoy conversations about making money. The next chapter isn't a get-rich strategy, but rather, one that has historically worked.

Age 47: Pile those Pennies

"Compound interest is the eighth wonder of the world. He who understands it, earns it . . . he who doesn't . . . pays it."

— Albert Einstein, German born physicist

I've never heard someone bragging about compounding returns at a ball game while spitting sunflower seeds.

Most money conversations are about stock picks and trading strategies. Unfortunately, egos only tell the stories of the rare winners and omit the price that was paid to get one positive return. Barber and Odean, who researched thirty-five thousand investors, found evidence of excessive trading that, rather than helped, actually reduced returns. Investors who focus on compounding, albeit boring and simple, have nothing to talk about at a social function. So we have choices; do we invest for the purpose of ego or do we do that which has proven to work over time? Here's how the idea of compounding works . . .

If you invest $1,000 and it returns 5 percent, you now have $1050. Then, the next year you earn interest on, not just your original deposit, but the entire $1,050. This happens year after year. Your interest earns interest on top of interest. It keeps going and doesn't quit.

A creative way to figure out compound interest in your head is called the rule of 72. Your money will double in ten years if you get an annual rate of return of 7.2 percent. Alternatively, if you earn 10 percent each year, your money will double in 7.2 years.

Memorize that rule and etch it into your brain as you try to build up twenty-five times your income for retirement.

Here's a compounding riddle from David Reiss, professor of law at Brooklyn Law School.

"Would you rather receive a gift on January 1 of $1 million or a penny that doubles every day for the rest of the month?"

The best answer? The penny doubler would finish the month of January with $9.7 million dollars! That's the power of compounding, and a riddle to share at your kid's next baseball game.

When your money begins to get compounding momentum, it will grow. And if you have piles of money, you must title it the right way, otherwise death, disability, or divorce could mess up a rather well-thought-out plan. That's the topic coming up.

Age 48: Titling Assets

"I told the banker that I'd like to set up a joint account with someone with lots of money."

— Unknown

Titling assets means that you will let a financial company know, very clearly, who is to receive your money if you were to pass away. I understand that this may be the most boring chapter in the book. But, you need to know about titling assets so your family can grieve without being frustrated or worried about funeral expenses, or—even worse—fighting over your money. Proper attention to titling resolves those post-death money issues.

The easiest and most convenient way to title your checking, savings, and investment accounts is called survivorship titling. An example would be John and Debbie Smith Joint Tenants with Rights of Survivorship (JTWROS). If John were to pass away, then Debbie would get access to the whole account.

The near opposite of JTWROS is often referred to as Joint Tenants in Common (JTEN). Different financial companies use different words and abbreviations, so you might see the letters JTEN, JTTEN, JTIC, or TENCOM after your name on a bank account. What this means is that you have told the financial company that just because somebody is a joint account owner, at your death, that person doesn't get your money. Sometimes this is the approach when an adult remarries and wants the child from the previous marriage to get the money. Just know that the money doesn't go automatically to the child. The child must bring in paperwork to the bank such as a death certificate and/or a will to confirm that it's his or her money.

If you want more control over the inheritance, you will need to set up a trust. How the account is titled determines how the assets are split, and the trust dictates to the bank where the assets go. The trust would be the beneficiary and the rules of the trust would specify who gets the money and how it is allocated.

There are a few times when you should pause and rethink titling outside the normal JTWROS.

1. When you are subject to the federal estate tax. In 2017, the federal estate tax exemption was $5.49 million. So, if your net worth at death is anywhere close this number, you should rethink titling. Life insurance proceeds could be considered in this calculation.

2. When you are subject to a state estate tax. As of 2017, there are fifteen states along with the District of Columbia that have an estate tax. Washington has the highest maximum estate tax rate at 20 percent. There are six states that have an inheritance tax. Regardless if it's estate or inheritance, it's a death tax and the bill must be paid.

3. You want privacy. If you want to ensure privacy from the probate process where your assets and liabilities are announced at the courthouse, you'll need to do a little more planning.

4. You want to customize how the kids get the money. Don't expect the banker to restrict your spendthrift son from cashing his inheritance check. This will take some legal work but it is usually worth the small investment.

5. You have real property. You may not want to be a joint beneficiary with someone else and, in turn, be a joint landlord or roommate.

The above exceptions are not an exhaustive list, but are rather a few of the more common reasons for doing more than the traditional

JTWROS. The rules can be a little tricky when non-spouses are involved, so be careful not to misstep when owning a joint account with your child or non-spouse. Of course, whenever, you are in doubt, hire a competent attorney to help navigate the complexities of titling assets.

Most of the time titling can be done at the bank, but sometimes it requires a conversation with an attorney. Speaking of hiring an attorney, you should probably hire a lot more people to help you get more done in life. I'll make a case in the next chapter that by hiring the right people at the right time in your life, you could save money, make money, and have a more fulfilling life.

Age 49: Outsourcing

"The successful warrior is the average man, with laser-like focus."

— Bruce Lee, actor and martial artist

According to Jayson DeMers in his article titled "7 Habits of the World's Richest People," 67 percent of the world's richest were cognizant of and careful how they spent their time.

We often think of outsourcing as only something you do in business and work. But the same principle of hiring someone to do a personal job so you can focus applies just as well.

I had a client tell me the other day, "You know, Darryl, the older I get the nicer it is to source things out."

I encourage you to diligently spend your life on what can be done well and hire others to do what isn't in your skill set. Outsourcing activities frees time so you can focus on what you are good at and what is important to you. And . . . it's how the rich get richer.

Some people refuse to outsource because they believe they are competent and can figure it out themselves. That is typically not true. In fact, the definition of hubris is excessive pride or self-confidence. It is because of hubris that many people (mostly men) refuse to outsource tasks.

Smart business people focus on what they are good at and outsource the rest. Figure out a way to do the same.

Outsourcing is only truly beneficial when it is replaced by time spent on something more valuable. For example, it would not be wise to outsource mowing the yard if you were to only play video games with the time saved. However, if someone else mowed your yard and you were allotted Saturday morning to coach your son's T-ball team, you have made a wise decision. Outsourcing and delegating should be done with the intent to focus on the activities that are much more valuable in life. Below is a list of everyday tasks to consider outsourcing.

1. Housekeeping
2. Lawn care
3. Auto maintenance
4. Administrative work (for entrepreneurs)
5. Taxes

Have you always wanted make a little money with a side hustle but never had time? If so, then outsource the projects you weren't made for and free up the hours to earn some extra cash! The math will tell you if it makes sense.

Done in a Decade
1. Purchased mutual funds and exchange-traded funds
2. Reestablished and stuck with a risk profile
3. Paid off all consumer debt
4. Set up a strict remodel budget
5. Hired college coach
6. Completed a deep financial checkup
7. Hired a competent CPA
8. Stuck with compound growth strategy
9. Titled assets properly
10. Outsourced other services

Age 50: No Time Left To Be Timid

"My biggest worry is I'm running out of time and energy. Thirty years ago I thought ten years was a really long time."

— Dean Kamen, American engineer and inventor

At this point in life you should intuitively know if you've been a good saver. Have you been disciplined or has life sucked away your paychecks? It is more effective to do the math, but many times, at age fifty, people know if they have saved up enough money for retirement. At age fifty, it's time to get serious about your wealth. Time is running out.

Don't expect your boss to bail you out. Any pay acceleration you might have enjoyed in your twenties, thirties, and forties is going to slow down considerably. In fact, according to the New York Fed, males' compensation hits a peak in the early to mid-fifties (the inflation-adjusted study focused on men because there is a degree of variability with women taking breaks from the workforce to care for children).

Don't expect to cash in on big pay bumps. You have to focus on other, more controllable ways of accumulating wealth.

For example, it's time that you reverse the lifestyle creep. For years, your lifestyle has become more expensive as your pay went up. Now, it's time to cancel expensive gym memberships, reduce the dining out, downsize another thousand square feet, and take budget vacations. Finally, stop justifying bad money decisions because you "have worked hard and earned it" or you "only live once."

Also, make sure to put on your oxygen mask before you put on your kid's mask. I know you want to help your children in life, but it is time for you to think about your future. If you are not careful about the amount of cash funding your adult children, put money boundaries in place today.

Now you should take at least half of every pay increase and put it in your IRA and 401(k). There is a reason that the Internal Revenue Service allows those over fifty to put more in their retirement accounts. In fact, they call it "catch up" because those in their fifties are often behind where they should be. Make it a goal to maximize your 401(k) and/or your IRAs.

Another smart, yet humbling, idea is to work part-time or have an after-hours consulting job. Working for Uber or Amazon is a popular way to accelerate your wealth if you don't spend the earnings. Consulting is attractive to employers because they get the benefit of your expertise without the obligations that come with hiring you as an employee. Also, because social security is based on the highest thirty-five years of earnings in your career, you will likely be increasing the amount of social security you receive in retirement.

Finally, if your employer offers tuition reimbursement—take it. Get the education needed to get a better career.

My point is this . . .don't expect material pay increases over the next ten to fifteen years to solve your financial problems. Take advantage of the health and energy you have today to accumulate wealth. If you can earn some extra cash and avoid impulse buying on gadgets and stuff, you will be able to accumulate the money needed to PIVOT. Let's talk about impulse buying in the next chapter.

Age 51: Shiny Short-Term Thinking

"Never let a short-term desire get in the way of a long-term goal."

— Curtis Martin, NFL Hall of Famer

I know what you're thinking. "I'm way behind on saving for retirement."

Even if it "feels" too late, it's not. There is still a good fifteen working years left in you. Let's make those earning years count. Those retirees who win with money establish long-term money goals and avoid distractions that pick at the plan.

I have a question: How many people who set New Year's goals never achieve them? The results are really bad. I'll tell you about them in a second.

But, why are we so bad at achieving our goals? Specifically our money goals?

It is mostly because we underestimate our lack of self-control and overestimate our ability to focus. It's tough to stay focused. Marketers are aggressively fighting for our credit and debit cards. They are shrewd.

But don't stop trying to beat American consumerism and adult peer pressure. Your family is counting on you to get better at focus and self-control.

Heidi Grant Halvorson, PhD, author of the book *Succeed*, suggested that, "self-control is learned, developed, and made stronger over time. If you want more self-control, you can get more. The same way you get bigger muscles by working out."

Being in your fifties, it's about that time in life to get serious about self-control money habits. In other words, we must make each day productive, reduce spending, and save aggressively.

To take it one step further, make a contract. Write it down, sign it, and give it to someone who will hold you accountable.

And don't be distracted by shiny things!

Sarah Stanley Fallaw, PhD, stated in her research report "Financial Behaviors & Wealth Potential" that "clients that focus intently on what others buy and consistently want the latest and greatest possessions (such as technology or accessories) are less likely to build wealth over time." This is the kind of shiny short-term thinking that will destroy your PIVOT plan.

These kind of distractions are why 92 percent of us fail at achieving our New Year's goals (University of Scranton).

Practice staying focused and developing your self-control muscle. If you fail, pick yourself back up and start over. This money discipline is not about win or lose, it's about win or learn.

Discipline with money is easy to say and hard to do, but certainly not impossible. It also is not impossible to reduce your taxes. You just need a strategy. The next chapter will address your PIVOT tax plan.

Age 52: Tax Diversification

"You don't pay taxes—they take taxes."
— Chris Rock, comedian

You know that putting all your eggs in one basket is a bad idea. What about putting all your eggs in the same tax basket? By diversifying your investments in different tax baskets, you will have more control over your retirement cash flow.

For example, when you retire, if you have investments that are *not* labeled IRA or 401(k), you will likely want to spend these monies first. The reason is that you will eventually spend the cost basis (what you put in). Because you don't pay taxes on what you put in, it reduces your overall taxable income. Reducing your taxable income then reduces the cost of Medicare and potential taxes on social security.

Next, you will take money out of the traditional IRAs and 401(k)s. By withdrawing from these accounts, you will reduce future required distributions at age seventy and a half.

Lastly, you will withdraw from the Roth IRAs. The PAX Financial Group team loves when you save the best for last because Roth IRAs are completely tax free and your kids can stretch this tax-free growth over time when they inherit it. The government hates Roth retirement withdrawals.

The above strategy is the ideal scenario. You may have a different game plan based on your situation. Regardless, start saving in different tax accounts now so when you retire, you'll have choices.

Spreading money around in three tax accounts will certainly help. But, be careful; you won't have enough to PIVOT if you overspend on your child's upcoming wedding.

Age 53: A Wise Wedding For Your Children

"Marriage. It's like a walk in the park. Jurassic Park."

— Unknown

How much would you guess an average wedding costs in America today? The answer may surprise you, and I'll share it with you in a moment.

First, I advise you to convince the lovebirds to take the cash and run. After that doesn't work, let's look at planning for the big event.

How do you enjoy the event, yet remain practical?

Does your second uncle's cousin get an invite to the wedding or is the venue too crowded to let him in? Should you invite all your daughter's coworkers, or just the ones you like? Where does the list stop?

According to *The Knot*, the average wedding costs $31,213! This means that only a few purchases might ever in your life (maybe a home or a car) exceed the price of a wedding.

The event is a big deal, but so is the price.

Now, if I put my financial planner hat on and look at the long-term impact of $31,000, I get an even more startling perspective. If you were to invest this money over forty years at a hypothetical 10 percent rate of return, your $31,000 would be over $1 million! Wow!

I digress. No one is going to convince a couple shot by Cupid to invest the proceeds of wedding money. If you do, can you negotiate a peace treaty between Israel and Iran?

Is there a way to get the big number down a little bit? Fewer guests might be the best starting point. The average number of guests for a wedding is 136. This means that you are spending $229 per guest. Don't think you're getting a return on that investment relative to the gift at the front door. Crock-Pots and toasters are not usually selling for $229. However, if you put a dollar value on each guest, you will think twice about adding your kid's high school art teacher to the invitation list. Additionally, if it's open bar, you might avoid everyone from your kid's old high school.

The most consistent theme I have seen over the years is the number of over-budgeted weddings. Why are weddings and home improvements always over budget? The reason is that they are often one-time events rarely practiced prior to execution. It's not as though a wedding plan happens every year. It's complex and we just don't have the experience. Also, it easy to justify luxury. The phraseology dad usually expresses is, "Well, I'm already in for twenty thousand dollars. What's another two thousand?" According to research, 23 percent of people don't even go in with a budget, so if you start with one, you deserve some credit!

My wife and I had the invitations for our wedding made at Kinko's. We made our own slideshow. We tried our best to be frugal and there is no doubt that memories were not diminished.

This is an emotional event. Pay attention to the details, and watch out for rip-offs like counterfeit dresses, incompetent wedding organizers, and extra fees in fine print.

If you want to be more accurate in your planning for a future wedding, head over to www.costofwedding.com and learn more about all of the unknowns that go into one of the most important days of your child's life.

If you paid for a wedding within reason, way to go! Now you can use your excess cash and consider investing in an annuity. But, you'll have to follow the specific annuity purchasing rules laid out in the next chapter.

Age 54: Annuities Might Work After All*

"People always live forever when there is an annuity to be paid to them."

— Jane Austen, English author

An annuity is an investment designed to provide an income that will last the rest of your life regardless of how long you live. It has a degree of complexity and a high cost.

I am a recovering annuity critic.

In 2008, I co-founded a radio show called "Financial Myth Busters." I spent much of my airtime bashing annuities, and for good reason. First, the annuities were pitched to people in a way that promised incredible investment performance without any risk. This sales approach was far from the truth. Salespeople with the education of a weekend life insurance exam discussed stock market related concepts. Then, add to these horrible sales practices, the commissions related to the sale of the products were so high that I developed a bitter taste for annuities.

Then, my thinking evolved. The collision of stock market fears, annuity product changes, and increased oversight focused on elderly protection helped change my perspective. Additional progress still needs to be made with annuities to establish them as a friendly investment option. However, today, PAX Financial Group has carefully identified the role annuities play in our clients' lives.

Because annuities haven't yet become entirely "friendly" to investors, proceed with prudence. Below are the only two reasons you should own annuities.

1. **Safety.** According to the 2013 Survey of Owners of Individual Annuity Contracts conducted by the Gallup Organization, most people purchased an annuity because of the perception that it was a "safe purchase." "Safety" should not be the primary motivation, because the thought is rooted in fear. Fear is an emotion and you should not make emotional investments. A purchase of an annuity for the purposes of avoiding market gyrations should only happen when you are absolutely losing sleep and considering the awful choice of cash as your long-term investment. Annuities can be a middle ground between cash and market-related investments but . . . they should be the last resort.

2. **Income.** The primary reason you should consider an annuity is guaranteed income. If you have a concern about living too long, then an annuity makes sense. An annuity company will typically guarantee you a paycheck regardless if the amount of money you gave the insurance company runs out.

Is it a good deal? It is not a good deal if you die too soon. It is a great deal if you live long. Don't worry. If you die too soon, unlike the old days, many insurance companies give the unused money back. But, if you live too long, the insurance company is on the hook for paying out money after you have spent all of yours. This is a situation the actuarial nerds of insurance companies want to avoid.

Think long and hard about living a long life. It happens. Don't dwell so much on your parents' life expectancy (although this is a factor), but rather consider this: the trend of life expectancy is increasing dramatically. Since 1970, the life expectancy of Americans has jumped from 70.8 years to seventy-nine years! If this trend continues, and you live too long, you will be very happy you own an annuity.

According to the 2013 Survey of Owners of Individual Annuity Contracts, the average age of an annuity purchase was younger than you might think . . . age fifty-one. But, don't jump in too quickly. Take your time and make sure you don't get sold on an emotional purchase. Even more importantly, don't invest "too much" in annuities. There is rarely a good reason to have more than 50 percent of your investable assets in an annuity due to surrender periods, fees, and complexity. However, annuities are an important part of the overall plan to protect you and your family from running out of money if you live too long.

An annuity is made so you won't outlive your money. But, major health care expenses could exceed the annuity check you are receiving. That health care threat requires uncomfortable, yet careful, thought. We'll unpack it in the next chapter.

*Fixed Annuities are long term insurance contacts and there is a surrender charge imposed generally during the first 5 to 7 years that you own the annuity contract. Withdrawals prior to age 59-1/2 may result in a 10% IRS tax penalty, in addition to any ordinary income tax. Any guarantees of the annuity are backed by the financial strength of the underlying insurance company.

Age 55: Long-Term Care Planning

"You know you're getting old when you can pinch an inch on your forehead."

— John Mendoza, author

I bet you just tried it.

According to the Department of Health and Human Services, almost 70 percent of people turning age sixty-five will need long-term care at some point in their lives.

Being from Texas, most of my big-hat and cattlemen usually say, "Put me out in the pasture . . . I ain't goin' to no nursing home."

I hear you . . . but your wife might need care.

Roughly two-thirds of the $6.6 billion in long-term care insurance claim benefits paid in 2011 were paid for women needing care.

While we still have all our marbles, it's time to think about and plan for the future. As far as I'm concerned, you have four choices to consider.

First, you could buy insurance, take the risk out of your life, and transfer it to a company in the business of paying for old people's bills. It's interesting to know that 65 percent of care doesn't last past ninety days because people either quickly recover or die. Also, the average length of stay is under three years. So, if you are going to get a long term care insurance policy, consider getting a ninety-day elimination, with a three-year benefit. PAX Financial Group always encourages our clients to purchase the inflation feature.

Second, you could depend on family to help. Unfortunately, most family is not living in the same cul-de-sac. In fact, 43 percent of grandparents live over 200 miles away from their grandchildren. That's a lot of gas and traffic separating the two. However, if you are blessed with family close by, make sure you talk about the uncomfortable game plan.

Third, you could use cash flow. If you are fortunate enough to have military retirement pay, teacher's retirement system retirement, a pension, social security, or some combination, you may in fact have the cash flow to cover the care you need. But put the math to the test; identify the cost of care and determine if your predictable income will cover the bills. Be sure to add a compounded 6 percent annual increase in health care costs. As you already know, this increase isn't provided on your income sources

Fourth, you could be broke. This is not an indictment on your character; this is just a strategy to play the game. The approach is to get rid of all your assets below the Medicaid level. Medicaid is a joint federal and state program that only pays for long-term care if you are indigent (i.e., broke). Don't be too discouraged; 49 percent of nursing home costs were covered by Medicaid by 2002. You will have to deplete your assets down to a low level and hand over all your paychecks to the nursing home. Then, you'll get the care you need.

If you are married, the probability is that one of you will need some help. Don't put your head in the sand. Start having the tough conversations about your long-term health today. Long-term care could wipe out a lifetime of savings. So could a divorce. That's why the topic made it in this book and in the next chapter.

Age 56: Divorce . . . Where Money Dies

"What is the easiest way to become a millionaire? Be a billionaire and get a divorce."

— Unknown

Have you heard that 50 percent of all marriages end in divorce? I know I spent much of my life believing this fact to be true. But is it true? Hang with me, in just a minute I'll give you an alternative statistic.

Divorce in general is rough but there is a demographic getting divorced at an alarming rate. The Society of Sociology at Bowling Green State University unpacked the divorce rate among baby boomers. The unsettling news is that the rate of divorce with this group has doubled since the 1990s.

Why is this so concerning? First, the only financial winners are those who make money to facilitate the divorce. The couples always lose money, typically thousands of dollars.

Other than the unfortunate unhealthy and abusive relationships, divorce among baby boomers is dangerous.

It's unfortunate that, as a financial advisor, I've been caught in the middle of mess and money and had to experience some of the emotions in divorce. I've received drunk calls from husbands, emotional emails from wives, and everything in between. But, my job is about money and I've kept my professional focus on the financial side. With that said, I can antidotally confirm the fast-paced divorce trend among baby boomers.

One of the first misalignments I have experienced is the disconnect between expectations and concerns. One spouse expects to travel while the other is worried about outliving the money. Or one spouse expects to move to cooler weather and the other is focused on health care where hospitals and physicians are the priority. Before retirement begins, expectations need to be aligned. If independent thoughts are not reconciled, couples could quickly move into covert coping, then frustration, and finally divorce.

This is where the financial impact comes in. After the attorney fees and legal costs there is the distribution of assets. The house is split in two and the 401(k) is cut in half. There are typically a few emotional missteps along the way, causing taxes and penalties, thus further draining the nest egg. Finally, when it's all settled, the divorced couple realizes that living on half of the income and half of the assets is not easier than expected. The joint effort that was considered leading up to retirement was a lot more comforting than the post-divorce financial outlook. In other words, it's expensive to pay for retirement alone.

Unfortunately, the financial impact of divorce isn't immediate. Twenty years down the road, the price of divorce will be painfully felt. It could literally lead one spouse to poverty.

According to the National Center for Health Statistics, for every one thousand people, there are 6.9 new marriages each year and 3.2 divorces. I suppose that if you take six and divide it by three, you'll get the 50 percent divorce rate we hear about. We are not at a 50% divorce rate, but those few who do divorce are in financial trouble.

My advice to most middle-class baby boomers: you've stuck it out this far, keep going because the financial impact is significant. It will be easier to work through life together, especially if you are providing support to kids and parents. People in this situation are considered the sandwich generation. We'll talk about strategy to survive the stress involved when caring for parents and children in our next chapter.

Age 57: Sandwich Generation

"Dear past, thanks for all the lessons. Dear future, I'm ready."
— PureHappyLife.com

According to a Pew Research study, one in seven middle-aged adults provides financial support to both a child and their aging parent.

If you're caring for parents, it's important to establish all money and non-money expectations with your brothers and sisters. For example, who is responsible for paying for home health care? Do mom and dad have enough cash flow or do we kids need to chip in? Who will take care of medical deductibles? Will each kid cover the bill equally? Should the richest of the children cover all the costs or should they be shared regardless of financial well-being? These are all difficult, yet important questions to discuss. Have an annual family meeting, keep good records, and don't keep any secrets.

Hopefully, with defined roles and responsibilities, all family members can chip in to help a little. If communication is respectable, it will bring the family closer and avoid petty disagreements. Ideally, the family attitude should not be rooted in discouragement but rather one of honor and loyalty to the parents.

It's hard enough to take care of parents, but when your kids need help at the same time, it creates even more strain on the wallet. Kids are moving back home after college or even after a few years of an unsuccessful career. It's a boomerang of bedrooms. Twenty-nine percent of young adults are now living with their parents.

"It's not fair, but it's fulfilling," recalled one of my sandwiched clients. She has to take care of her eighty-five-year-old mother's finances, doctor visits, and random requests. Because there were not clearly defined and agreed upon roles, there was a degree of resentment with a brother who lives up north and sister who lives at the beach. But, she will not let that frustration bring them down.

To take it one step further, her adult daughter moved back in because the daughter is going through a nasty divorce.

This client is sandwiched in the golden years. She is sandwiched between adult children with life challenges and aging parents.

She's not alone. This is the new normal of many Americans.

If you don't hold a family meeting someone will hold a family grudge. When in this sandwiched position, it is critical to define the roles and responsibilities of everyone involved. Siblings who are caring for their parents can get overwhelmed and bitter, not because they are bad people, but because of the stress and burden of caregiving.

It isn't going to be easy, but with the right attitude, team, and realistic expectations . . . it will be fulfilling.

When sandwiched between kids and parents, stress levels go up, and decisions are made on emotions. Train yourself now to manage your investments the right way. That training is a major topic of our next chapter.

Train Yourself

A Michigan lady saved a four-year-old child from the bottom of the pool. The little boy was completely blue and no longer breathing. She said that while performing CPR, she had to "zone in and just do what we were trained."

A man in Massachusetts was surrounded by flames and smoke on the porch of his apartment. Two firefighters climbed over the railing and pulled the man toward the balcony's edge. The success was because, according to the firefighters, "We fell back on our training and the ladder was raised and the rescue was made very quickly."

The Secret Service Agent Jerry Parr, who pushed President Reagan into a limousine and out of the way of additional rounds of fire, says his training to "cover and evacuate" took over.

You are in a point in life where your money is or will start having zeros at the end of it. Much of the content of the book is designed to help train you for the inevitable freighting and emotional events of the future.

Age 58: Investment Statement Risk

"Some things just aren't meant to go together. Things like oil and water. Orange juice and toothpaste."

— Jim Butcher, author

Today, Jack and Jill each have wealth of $5 million dollars. Yesterday, Jack had $1 million and Jill had $9 million. Are they equally happy? There is no right answer, but this question has psychologists buzzing with research, surveys, and test groups. However, one thing is clear: emotions and money are not independent of each other.

Unfortunately, monthly investment statements deliver more than investment numbers. They also deliver emotions tied to losses and gains.

In a study performed by behavioral finance expert Richard Thaler, two groups were given hypothetical portfolios. One group received performance feedback monthly, while the other group received performance feedback annually. The "monthly group" received negative reports 39 percent of the time. While the "annual group" received negative reports 14 percent of the time.

When Thaler asked the participants at the end of the study, "How would you invest your money?" The monthly group said they would only put 40 percent of their money in stocks while the annual group said they would put 70 percent of their money in stocks.

In other words, the monthly group became timid solely on the frequency of information. This fear deceived them and impacted their investment approach.

There are two practical ways you can avoid being deceived by your investment statements.

First, don't reference the high water mark in your investments every time you gaze at a statement. In other words, don't say, "It was at one hundred thousand dollars last month and now it's down to ninety thousand dollars. It's a trend! I'm losing money!" High water marks are nice, but they should not be the permanent point of reference. Our team at PAX Financial Group often takes clients back to their initial investment so they are reminded of the starting point in their investment journey.

Second, check on your investments less frequently. The most frequent you should review your long-term investment plan is quarterly. Daily watching can lead to knee-jerk buys and sells that result in permanent investment losses.

If you follow these two simple rules you will minimize the risk of your statements mixing your money with your emotions. By the way, I feel PIVOTing is happening very soon. Let's get serious about our PIVOT in the next chapter.

Age 59: The Time Has Come To PIVOT

"When quitting is done correctly, it isn't giving up – it's making room for something better."

— Adam Kirk Smith, author

If you are exhausted and disengaged at work, you are not alone. Do you know how many baby boomers are frustrated with work? I'll tell you in a few seconds.

Just know that if you are discouraged, you aren't helping your employer, coworkers, or your health, and it may be time to move on to the next season of life.

Here are five reasons why you should retire now:

1. You are cynical. You are no longer willing to invest the hours to tackle a big project. You find projects to be a waste of energy and have experienced too many failures in the past to muster up hope in the next one.

2. You are tired. You are working slowly. You love long water-cooler conversations that sweep you away from your job. You find stress-relieving activities are more frequent than goal-achieving activities.

3. You are no longer valuable in your role . . . ouch. Everyone around you is doing the heavy lifting. Yes, your seniority is nice and sometimes useful, but the team is solid. You may have noticed the request for your help is less frequent than in the past. You know who would succeed you if you left and, believe it or not, they are anxiously waiting for the promotion.

4. You have other interests. You spend more time researching golf, wine, traveling, arts, sports, woodwork, or any other hobbies. You have moved from amateur to semi-professional expert in your hobby. You know your stuff and can even bring value to your community at trade shows, part-time work, or through community leadership. As a matter of fact, your friends and peers in the community can't wait to hang out with you a little more.

5. Your health is deteriorating. The stress of the job along with the demands of corporate America or government regulation are taking their toll. Your blood pressure is up and your back is hurting. You don't move around as much and you feel sluggish. Caffeine is the only substance that gets you through the day.

According to a Gallup report, nearly one in four baby boomers are actively disengaged in work. It is not uncommon to find unhappy workers in America today.

If you find one of the five reasons listed above tapping you on your shoulder, don't be afraid. Be honest with yourself. It's time to move on to something bigger and even better. It is time to PIVOT!

Done in a Decade
1. Identified other ways to earn money
2. *Rebalanced your investments
3. Established tax diversification
4. Developed a mature buying approach that avoids "shiny" things
5. Considered purchasing an annuity
6. Established a long-term care plan
7. Sought marital counseling
8. Identified the frequency of reviewing investments
9. Facilitated family meeting about parents' care
10. Considered when to officially retire

*Rebalancing can entail transaction costs and tax consequences that should be considered when determining a rebalancing strategy.

SECTION II: PIVOT

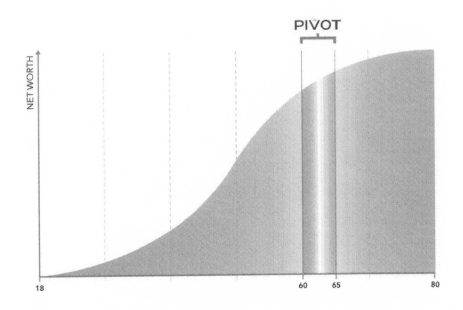

I laugh out loud when I think of Michael Scott from the hit TV show, *The Office*. He and his girlfriend made some outrageous financial purchases and were completely broke. Michael learned that his best solution was to declare bankruptcy. So, he decided to humble himself and pursue what he considered his only option. As a result, he walked into the cubical room from the kitchen and screamed, "I declare . . . BANKRUPTCY." A few minutes later, his company accountant pulled him aside and said, "You just can't 'declare' bankruptcy."

I share that story because Michael Scott turned off his thinking hat and moved forward with unprepared action. I would suggest to you that the number-one key to a successful retirement is preparation. If you don't prepare well, peer pressure, QVC, and con artists will tell you how to spend your retirement money.

You can do this retirement thing. You just need to invest the time in the next five years simulating retirement both with money and behavior. This means practicing your spending, understanding your investment plan, aligning your family expectations, and avoiding the money influence from marketing and neighbors.

I've enjoyed the degree of accuracy and consideration from my client, Jeff, when he left his twenty-five-year position in accounting from a big oil company. He thought about nearly everything and made not one quick and irrational judgement. My clients Mark and Sarah evaluated where in the United States (all options on the table) they were going to live and what they were going to do after they both retired from successful leadership careers. Their exploration led to a renewed enthusiasm for life.

Whenever a family takes time to carefully evaluate their plan, the risks, and the opportunities, they can "chillax." They can actually watch the sunrise and sip on a cup of coffee without anxiety. Alternatively, those who don't plan well, drink that cup of coffee with the noise of the market in the background. They wake up to daily anxiety-whispering images of becoming an old man or old woman forced to declare . . . **BANKRUPTCY!**

Age 60: Don't Retire . . . PIVOT

"What do you call a person who is happy on Monday? Retired."

— Author unknown

Throw out the idea of retirement and consider "PIVOTing" in life. Retirement is defined as "the disposition of an asset over its useful life." Is your life no longer useful? Let's consider this season to be a time where you PIVOT to a new experience that could (with the right intentionality) make a difference in your life and others.

Are you curious what the PIVOT acronym is? I think it's cool, but first let me tell you how to get you, your family, and your money positioned to PIVOT.

1. **Pay off consumer debt.** Not only should you get rid of the interest and payments, you should reduce the stress associated with the *pesky payments*. If you do, you'll have the cash flow to spoil your grandkids.

2. **Pay off mortgage.** If this requires you to downsize or move, then make it happen. Pay off the line of credit you took out to pay for your kid's college. Get the mortgage balance to zero. You should not go into your retirement years with a mortgage.

3. **Practice living on a PIVOT retirement budget.** This is important. A Gallup poll reported that Americans spend the most on Saturday. Well, when you retire, every day is a Saturday. Separate your cash flow into two groups: *needs and wants*. Then, monitor spending in each broad category.

4. **Account for replacement expenses.** Start to identify how frequently you will need to upgrade vehicles. When do you suppose you will need a new roof? When accounting for replacement expenses, either set aside the money each month or plan on making a major withdrawal from your investments in the future.

5. **Evaluate pension options and survivorship options.** Consider establishing a pension maximization plan while healthy. This means that instead of getting a 75 percent survivorship option on your pension, you elect to buy life insurance. This isn't always the right way to go, but if you don't run the math while you are healthy, a door of choice will close.

6. **Identify a list of activities and start practicing.** If you are married, align interests so you don't drift away. Find common ground and start practicing. Will you be active or quiet? Will you do ministry work or will you start a business? Don't wait to figure this out when you have the extra time to kill each other.

7. **Determine a giving strategy.** Will you give while alive or will you give when you die? If you practice PIVOT now, you will not stress over something so impactful. Here's a hidden truth . . . those who haven't run the retirement numbers are so concerned with running out of money, they are afraid to cash the giving ticket.

8. **Practice risk.** When you have more free time, you will study your investments more closely. Statement anxiety only rewards you with high blood pressure. PAX Financial Group helps our clients establish their tolerance for investment volatility. Tolerance takes effort and practice. Be sure to clearly define what "risk" means to you.

Stress test the PIVOT plan *five years* before the date of your departure from work. Stress test by asking the questions: What if we live longer than we expect? What would happen if inflation occurs? How would we handle a big health care expense? Discuss the odds and the impact.

PIVOT stands for:

Peace,

Imagination

Vigor,

Opportunity and

Time.

At age sixty, odds are you still have a lot of time left. According to the Department of Labor, the average American spends roughly twenty years in retirement. With that much life left, let's PIVOT the right way.

If you get a ticket to PIVOT, you will want to know exactly how money gets from investments into your bank account just as if you were employed. That is the topic in our next chapter.

Bonus Chapter

You may have questions about how to professionally notify human resources about your upcoming retirement. Go to this link and grab a bonus chapter: www.paxfinancialgroup.com.

There, you will find information on how to professionally notify your company of your upcoming retirement.

Age 61: The Mechanics Of IRA Deposits

"Carpe per diem—seize the check."

— Robin Williams, actor

Retirement is near. You are anxiously waiting for the time to replace an employment check with a retirement check. The question our clients at PAX Financial Group always ask is, "How does the process of getting a check actually work?"

Here's the normal process . . . first, you will need to determine the amount of money you want "net" of income taxes (after income taxes). To calculate the after-tax amount, take the dollar amount of income and divide it by (1 minus your tax bracket).

For example:

Let's say Maria wants $1,000 per month from her IRA. She would request a distribution from her financial institution in the amount of $1,250 ($1,000/(1-.20)). The .20 is equivalent to 20 percent and the most common tax scenario. However, if you are in a higher tax bracket you may need to increase the withholding to 25 percent or 30 percent. The formula will work the same.

Then, make sure you tell the financial institution the exact amount of the gross distribution (how much you want to have withheld), and what amount you will expect to hit your bank account.

Next, the financial institution (bank, insurance company, investment firm) will send the withholding directly to the IRS and you will settle up when you file your tax return. Hopefully, the amount you withheld is more than needed so you won't be faced with a balance due. If you want to be more accurate, you can always navigate to the IRS site and find your personal bracket.

Finally, you will need to provide the financial institution your bank routing number and account number. They will typically submit the transfer of funds through an Automated Clearing House (ACH) directly to your bank account. You can also set it up where they make this transaction every month so you can expect a deposit in your bank just as you did when you were working.

Once everything is set up, you can change the withholding, amounts, or banking information at any time. Of course, the less you mess with it, the more you can relax. The more you relax, the more you are free to fly around the country (on a budget of course).

IRA deposits combined with social security should be a significant part of your income. But should you take social security now? I'll answer that question in the next chapter.

Age 62: Let Your Social Security Cook*

"Social Security is the very foundation of retirement security for millions of Americans."

— Sue Kelly, member of the United States House of Representatives

As you blow out sixty-two candles, you will find yourself googling social security strategies. The big decision is, "Should I take it now or later?" Below are the following four reasons why you should let your social security check cook until age seventy.

First, you get an 8 percent annual pay increase each year you wait. Can you think of anywhere else where you would get this risk-free rate of return on your money? This means that your social security check will be 132 percent of what you might have received at full retirement age.

Second, headlines scream that social security is broke but the chances of you getting your check is still very high. To affirm that you won't get your benefit is pure speculation until evidence to the contrary is announced. The reality is that the benefactors of social security go to the voting booth and a lower check will not play well in Washington.

Third, your spouse will get your higher payout. Should you die before your spouse, generally, your spouse will get your greater check. Unfortunately, your spouse won't get both. But, by waiting, you are helping your widow make ends meet much easier.

Finally, you are living longer. Modern medicine coupled with hygiene and safety awareness are advancing rapidly. Don't bet against advancing longevity. A higher paycheck later in life will be helpful.

Of course, there are always exceptions to the "let your social security check cook" rule of thumb. Begin with the premise that delaying social security is the right choice until you find the evidence that confirms otherwise.

Social security is challenging but, frankly, is way more black and white than the next conundrum—how you manage your investment portfolio during PIVOT.

*Not associated with or endorsed by the Social Security Administration or any other government agency.

Age 63: Switching Money Lanes

"Investing should be more like watching paint dry or watching grass grow. If you want excitement, take eight hundred dollars and go to Las Vegas."

— Paul Samuelson, American economist

When someone is frustrated with the stock market, usually, it's not the stock market that's the problem. The market has proven to work over time. The real problem is you and me. The reason . . . we mess with our money too much. We act like a car in traffic, making futile attempts to get ahead by constantly switching lanes. Much of our job at PAX Financial Group is to help people not switch lanes at the wrong time.

We humans are gullible. We hear about two plane crashes in the last month and decide to drive instead of catching a more logical flight. Did the odds change? Nope, but we make the silly assumption that planes are all of a sudden more dangerous and we readjust our decision-making. Experts call this decision-making "availability bias." According to phycologist Jonathan Hadith, "The emotional tail wags the rational dog."

This emotional decision-making is the number one enemy of successful investing.

Sometimes emotions cause us to make bets on the direction of the market or a sector. Other times we make the unmerited mistake of looking at last year's winners and shift money their direction. Sometimes we simply rebalance too much.

In full disclosure, the historical returns of the S&P 500 stocks are not certain and you can't guarantee them. However, as long as people globally are shopping on Amazon, ordering grande vanilla lattes, watching another *Fast and Furious*, buying toilet paper, exchanging tires, and purchasing medicine, then the stock market is likely to go up.

The biggest challenge for investors is not the stock market, but rather, messing around with long-term investments because of boredom, hunches, or speculation masked in half-truths. Don't try to outsmart the market. Stick to the plan.

React vs. Respond

When dealing with money and markets it is critical that you know the difference between a reaction and a response.

A reaction is instant, unconscious, and often a defense mechanism. It's full of juice that makes you feel.

A response takes into consideration the well-being of not only you today, but your future self and others around you.

Reactions can result in expensive money mistakes. Much of the content in this book is designed to help you respond, not react, to money challenges.

Age 64: Retirement Could Kill You

"The two most important days in your life are the day you were born and the day you find out why."

— Mark Twain, writer and humorist

Retirement talk involves much more than money. Why? Two major threats to money are longevity and health. What impacts longevity and health? Many factors including lifestyle, community, and purpose. So, for us to be successful in our PIVOT, we need to take the retirement conversation beyond investments and money.

Imagine you are on a ladder, and the first rung has the number "zero" painted on it and the top rung has the number "ten" painted on it. The top rung, number ten, is the best possible life you could have right now with community, vigor, and hope. The bottom rung is the worst life you could have and represents loneliness, poor health, and despair.

Right now, what rung are you on? Really pause and give yourself a number before moving on. It's important for our conversation.

Let me be clear, if you are near the bottom of the ladder, retirement will magnify your existing challenges. Those at the bottom and deciding to retire are significantly increasing their chances of having a heart attack, stroke, or becoming clinically depressed.

But there is hope.

With intentional thought and action designed around developing a purpose in retirement, we find life.

According to a 2016 special *Time* edition called *The Science of Happiness* people who are more optimistic or have a *greater sense of purpose* have at least a 20 percent reduced risk of developing a major illness such as coronary heart disease or diabetes.

Let's kick this despair in the butt and move up the ladder. Here's what we've got to do before we actually retire . . .

1. Take inventory of your past. I'm inspired when I read about presidents. I'm not in love with the position, but it is the one place I can learn about folly and success served in history but delivered in biography. You have a biography too. There will be a time when your biography will inspire others.

2. Identify your gifts. We all have something we're good at. Unfortunately, because we are not perceived to be the best or haven't been publicly recognized for our gifts, we become insecure. Don't let this insecurity stop you. A good gift today is better than a great gift that never lived.

3. Assess what makes you cry. The CEO of World Vision, Richard Stearns said, "Lord, break my heart for what breaks yours." If you find something that makes you cry, lean into that cause. This is where passion is found. People and ideas are rarely moved by intellect. They are mostly moved by passion. If you have passion for something, you are needed.

4. Share with others. There is wisdom in the counsel of advisors. Make sure you take some quality time with others to address the concerns you have and to acknowledge what tugs at your heart. The candid nature of your peers will refine your approach.

5. Start with your neighbor. If you want to change the world, start with your neighbor. Build relationships in your community as a stepping stone. You will find that geographic location of your endeavors bridged with common relationships will make your purpose easier. A purposeless

retirement is no joke. I've seen very wealthy people decay solely because they traded their purpose for golf clubs. According to a report by the Institute of Economic Affairs, retirement increases the risk of clinical depression by 40 percent. Those in the second half of life have experience and wisdom; now it's time to deploy it. Our world needs this gift. So do you.

SECTION III: PURPOSE

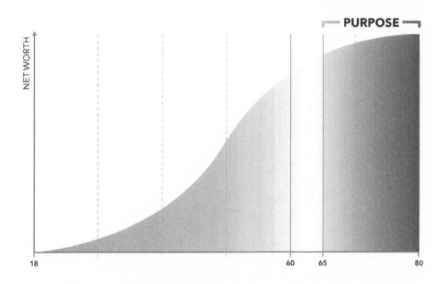

Question: A man takes his car to a hotel. Upon reaching the hotel, he is immediately declared bankrupt. Why? I'll finish the riddle in a moment. First, are you pessimistic that your retirement money will be met with the same bankruptcy fate? Or, do you have the optimism of good health, rainbows, and unicorns? Maybe your perspective is somewhere in between, in the land of hopeful, realistic optimism.

PURPOSE is retirement life that includes the go-go years, the so-so years, and the no-go years. All the years have threats. For example, how will we pay for health care? If we have cognitive declines, how do we protect our money from being influenced by "buy now" Amazon temptations? In the next section we will discuss the probabilities of threats and identify ways to insure, outsource, or retain the risks.

The opportunities outweigh the threats! I love what Mary decided to do as she was in the PURPOSE stage of her life. She sold her real estate holdings, simplified, and created blank space to enjoy time traveling with friends and family. David and Jessica struggled to find purpose but took the risk to open an art studio and a fly-fishing guide service. Now they interact with the local community like never before.

Pre-retirement people knew their purpose was to raise kids, work hard, love their spouse, or serve others. Life is different when you retire. It is time to develop a new purpose.

As you can see, this PURPOSE life is full of questions that can be categorized into threats and opportunities. Unlike our man in the riddle who filed bankruptcy at the hotel, retirement is not a game of MONOPOLY. There is no second chance.

Our goal in PURPOSE is to be real about the threats and take advantage of the opportunities. We will discuss the most salient issues that exist from age sixty-five to age eighty. Of course, you are more than welcome to live beyond age eighty, and the odds are . . . you will.

Age 65: Medicare

"When you're sick, you present your Medicare card, not your credit card . . ."

— Jack Layton, Canadian politician

According to the Congressional Budget Office, the cost of Medicare is 14 percent of our overall federal budget. But, despite the miscalculations of the past and the adjustments needed in the future, Medicare is here to stay. Below are ten key points to know about Medicare:

1. You sign up for Medicare at age sixty-five. You get a window to sign up three months before your birthday, the month of your birthday, and three months afterward. Put it on your calendar now.

2. Medicare covers non-custodial claims. Medicare covers broken bones and doctor visits, not nursing home costs. That's a different type of insurance called Long Term Care Insurance.

3. Medicare is not Medicaid. Medicaid is a health insurance program designed for those who are indigent. There is a financial qualification to get Medicaid and the benefits are different than for those on Medicare. Most retirees are on Medicare.

4. Part A is to pay for the hospital visits. You will have a deductible and this deductible amount changes each year.

5. Part B is to pay for the doctors' visits. You will have to pay a small deductible, then 20 percent of the costs up to a maximum out of pocket.

6. Part D is to pay for drugs. Make sure you check the drug list for each plan before you enroll.

7. Medicare Advantage Plans are a private health insurance alternative to government Medicare. About 30 percent of beneficiaries use Medicare Advantage plans.

8. If you are receiving social security, the cost of Medicare will come out of your social security check.

9. The cost of Medicare depends on your income. If you have a high retirement income, you and your spouse could be paying almost $800 per month for this coverage.

10. You can change most coverage once per year, usually in the fall.

Health insurance can be tricky. But, the Medicare market, as of late, has been kind to our retirees. As long as you check your doctors and drugs before you sign up, you should be okay. If you did make a mistake, you can adjust it each year.

As I said before, Medicare is here to stay. But what about social security? I'll answer that in the next chapter.

Age 66: Odds of Getting Social Security

"More young people believe they'll see a UFO than they'll see their own social security benefits."

-Mitch McConnell, American politician

Even those who watch more *Survivor* than CNBC know that Social Security is bankrupt. But, people are still paying in and benefits haven't stopped, so we have to ask ourselves, can we count on it?

Using the Congressional Budget Office's five hundred distribution of outcomes, you can get some degree of unemotional probabilities.

Someone who was born in the 1960s has a 98 percent probability of receiving most of his or her social security. "Most," by definition is 80 percent or more of what is promised on the green statements. It is safe to say that you can count on social security even though it may feel like social insecurity.

I know you are worried about social security, and I know you also worry about your parents' finances. The next chapter will address some of the most salient threats to their money.

Age 67: Financial Questions to Ask Your Elderly Parents

"Lying and stealing are next-door neighbors."

— A proverb

Can you guess, out of ten senior citizens, how many have been the target of fraud over the past year? Before I answer that question, let me remind you that you have parents with a target on their back. Before it is too late, make sure you ask the following four questions about who is advising them about money.

1. What is their professional background? Don't just take their word for it. PAX Financial Group found out a few years ago that an advisor in our community blatantly lied on his website about his resume. Later he ended up in jail for fraud. If you want the facts about the person's professional history, go to the Financial Industry Regulatory Association website at http://www.finra.org/ or look at the bottom of the advisor's website for a form called ADV. There are a handful of helpful disclosures on this document.

2. Who is the custodian of the money? The custodian is similar to a bank account. If the custodian is a household name like Charles Schwab, LPL Financial, Edward Jones, or TD Ameritrade, you likely can rest assured. However, if the custodian is the financial advisor or a company you are not familiar with, it is important to ask questions to ensure that the money has not been commingled with the advisor's personal funds.

3. How much of their money is in an annuity? Annuities, by themselves, are not bad. However, the products have historically been abused by salespeople. A wrong recommendation could tie up someone's money for an absurd about of time (ten years). There should be a valid strategy for an annuity recommendation and you should ensure that no more than 50 percent of their money is in annuity.

4. Are they too aggressive? When the market continues to accelerate to all-time highs, someone sitting at home watching CNBC all day can manufacture a belief that they can beat the market. I have seen cases where greed colliding with poor advice sprinkled with leverage can destroy someone's wealth. Make sure that the individual stocks and bonds they're recommending are not high-risk bets. Start asking questions if the individual stocks are above 20 percent of the portfolio.

Senior citizen abuse takes many forms and financial abuse is one that doesn't get enough attention. The two regulatory bodies that govern our industry (FINRA and SEC) have made it a point to dig deep in the audits of financial advisors to ensure that the elderly are properly guided. However, not all crooks are caught. It's important that you, as a family member, ask tough questions for the benefit of someone you love.

Yes, there is a lot to think about right now. The stock market is certainly one of them. However, at this age you shouldn't worry to the point of losing sleep. That's what I'll address next.

Age 68: Chillax

"There's always something to worry about."

— **Hersh Cohen, Co-chief Investment Officer at ClearBridge Investments**

How do you know if your worry is real or just manufactured by Facebook posts, email forwards, CNBC headlines, or a brother-in-law who knows someone who works in the CIA who knows something about what is going to happen sometime?

Below are four ways your worry may be in vain.

1. The market goes down by 5 percent. Since 1927, the S&P 500 has averaged a correction of at least 5 percent about once every three and a half months. A pullback is as normal and predictable as a wave crashing or the sun rising.

2. You only read the headline. In March of 1972, the *Time* magazine cover asked, "Is the U.S. Going Broke?" In January of 1991, *Time's* headline stated, "High Anxiety." In July of 2003, *Time* asked its readers on the cover, "Will You Ever Be Able To Retire?" If you could time travel would you go back and invest $100,000 in 1972, 1991, or 2003? We can't sue headlines for negligent advice, so be acutely aware that they mislead without consequences.

3. Investment salespeople who are consistently negative are considered bears. Someone who always claims that the market will crash will eventually be right . . . one day. It is easier to convince the consumer that the market will crash and sell the solution. The problem is that it could take years for the "theory"

to develop, and until then, there's a price to pay for pessimism. Ask the bear mogul about his track record. That might make him go into hibernation.

4. There are lines at Starbucks. Consider the global demand. The global middle class in India, China, Russia, Brazil, and many other countries want what the West has today. They are buying toothpaste, steaks, tires, toilet paper, and iPhones. If you need to be convinced, look at the lines for overpriced coffee and it's clear that we are a far cry from food rationing.

Yes, the market could crash. But, it's a possibility, not a probability. Maybe this worry stuff is a waste of energy. Like my son tells me, "Dad, chill." Relax. Chillax.

The capital markets will still be around to support your long-term goals. If they continue to grow, you will need to develop a legacy plan so you don't leave the next generation worse than you found it. That's the topic of our next chapter.

The Porch

If someone isn't taking huge risks and is well diversified, I believe if and when the market goes down they will fall off the porch, not the roof. In other words, they will experience some paper losses but not to the extreme of others who are taking big bets.

I would suggest that you ask your advisor . . .
"Based on how I am invested, if the market goes down dramatically, will I fall off the porch or will I fall off the roof?"

Age 69: Updating Wills

"Death ends a life, not a relationship."

— Jack Lemmon, American actor and musician

"I keep putting off my will." This is a phrase we hear nearly every day at PAX Financial Group. Don't let these be your famous last words. It's time to put down on paper who's receiving your money and how they get it.

Unfortunately, you are not alone. According to a recent Gallup poll, more than 50 percent of people don't have a will.

When you die without a will, it's considered "intestate" and it's the responsibility of the state to decide who gets your money. The late rocker Prince died intestate and we may see a decades-long legal battle. He died without a spouse, children, or parents. There are multiple siblings and half siblings staking claim to his multimillion dollar estate.

When you sit down with the attorney, they'll take a few minutes and educate you on the probate process and the role the will plays in helping you during this difficult time (in full disclosure they aren't helping you . . . you're dead).

Then, the attorney will likely ask, "Who do you want as a beneficiary?" Of course, you'll answer, "My spouse and then my kids." This order makes sense, but only if your kids act like adults. What if your kids misbehave or marry someone who misbehaves? In the spirit of not knowing the future behavior of your beneficiaries, it's important to establish future boundaries. Money will accentuate behavior . . . good or bad.

Remember, an inheritance is what you leave "to" someone. A legacy is what you leave "in" someone.

Done in a Decade
1. Established PIVOT buckets
2. Set up new paycheck strategy
3. Defined social security plan
4. Established rebalance plan (again)
5. Developed purpose and community in retirement
6. Purchased Medicare
7. Reevaluated social security plan (if necessary)
8. Checked on parents' financial well-being
9. Developed mental toughness regarding market volatility
10. Updated wills

Age 70: Required Minimum Distributions (RMDs)

"Money in the bank is like toothpaste in the tube. Easy to take out, hard to put back."

— Earl Wilson, former professional baseball player

At age seventy and a half, the IRS blows out candles not only to celebrate your half birthday but also the taxes you'll pay from Required Minimum Distributions (RMDs) on your IRAs.

Although RMDs are generally unavoidable, below are some helpful ideas to help navigate the inevitable RMD date.

1. Don't double up. You have a choice in your first RMD year to delay your withdrawal until the following year. Rarely does this make sense. When you delay your withdrawal you have twice as much to pull out of your IRA in year two. Not only does this create extra income tax but it could also affect your social security and Medicare.

2. Don't expect the bank to help. If your money is held at a bank or with another financial custodian, don't expect them to make the withdrawal for you. The institution is only obligated to notify you, not execute the actual RMD. PAX Financial Group tries our best to help with RMDs but the final obligation lies with the IRA owner.

3. Don't forget. If you forget to take your RMD, you will pay a 50 percent tax penalty. Ouch.

4. Know the calculation method. The IRS takes a snapshot of your IRA balance the year before you turn seventy and a half, and every year after that. This is the value used for the calculation. Then, in your first RMD year, divide the prior year-end balance by 27.4. This will be your first-year RMD. Keep in mind a few key points: (a) the IRS can change this number periodically; (b) the number will be different for each age; and (c) it will be different under alternative beneficiary scenarios.

5. Give to charity. You can give your RMD directly to charity. If you don't give it directly, you will have to pay income tax on the RMD and then only *possibly* get a charitable income tax deduction. Charitable deductions are itemized deductions so if you are like most Americans who use the standard deduction, then you won't even get to offset the withdrawal against a deduction. By sending the RMD check directly to your favorite nonprofit you can be assured of no income tax due.

6. Convert before seventy and a half. You have a few years prior to age seventy and a half to convert your traditional IRA to a Roth. If you strategize, you can reduce the amount required to come out each year because Roth IRAs don't have RMDs.

The RMD game is relatively straightforward once you get started. It's the initial withdrawal that requires a little planning. If you end up working in retirement, you may find yourself not even spending your RMD. At your age, there are still a few solid employment opportunities. I'll share those with you next.

Age 71: If You're Not Dead, You're Not Done

"Almost everything will work again if you unplug it for a few minutes, including you."

— Anne Lamott, American novelist

The retirement honeymoon is over and the idea of running out of money sets in. While you still have some brain and energy left, you consider outside work.

You are not alone in this way of thinking. In a joint study conducted by Bank of America, Merrill Lynch, and Age Wave, nearly half of retirees today either have worked or plan to work in retirement.

It's a smart move! The part-time work take the pressure off of investment withdrawals and allows them to cook longer.

The obstacles for retirees to work are not insurmountable. With brick-and-mortar businesses under financial pressure, e-commerce has filled in the gaps. The barrier to entry for entrepreneurs has dropped dramatically. The ability to be an Uber driver or Amazon deliverer is relatively easy. Studies show that many new entrepreneurs today are seniors. You can be a part of this positive trend!

Living a long life is possible and your window to earn a few more dollars is now. Take advantage of your energy and wits while you have them. We don't know what tomorrow holds. This extra cash could be the financial lifeline for your future self.

The funny thing about working is that you will spend less time watching the news and the stock market scares. But, if you still catch a glance at the headlines, quickly put them in context with the information in the next chapter.

Age 72: The Escalator

"The four most dangerous words in investing are 'This time it's different.'"

— Sir John Templeton, investor, banker, and fund manager

Why you should rethink your "market crashing" theory . . .

One of the most frequent questions we hear at PAX Financial Group when the market has a little dip is, "Is this the big one all over again?!" The "big one" is a reference to the 2008 crash. We all have scars from that year. When you become concerned, you will then find yourself accepting, ever so subtly, the same scary whisper from every corner of your life. This frequent repetition becomes familiar, and makes it hard to distinguish from the truth.

The truth is that market dips are normal and expected. But they do feel a little different today. It may help you in your investment strategy to understand that *the market is like a child with a yo-yo on an escalator.*

The yo-yo is volatility. The yo-yo is all the ups and downs and all the downs and ups. Today, the yo-yo is the combination of the following four new market normals:

1. High-Frequency Trading - These are computers that trade at a rapid pace and attempt to make money through the compounding of small wins. These companies will go as far as to pay a premium for high bandwidth to get an edge.

2. Retail Traders - The age of E-Trade and Schwab is a positive. But the indirect consequence is a massive increase in visibility

and access. When retail investors see volatility, they will react with emotion (generally . . . I'm not talking about you).

3. Algorithm Trading - These are computer models used by financial advisors and other institutions. They give a green light to buy and a red light to sell. When all the red lights go off at the same time, everyone sells.

4. Exchange-Traded Funds (ETFs) - These are like mutual funds but they can be sold in the middle of the day (whereas mutual funds can only be sold at market close). If the noise of the media gets too loud, everyone reacts in unison and sells their ETFs right after lunch, causing more market volatility.

You could place some blame of recent stock market volatility on the above four new market normals. But, I wouldn't worry about them too much. Those four are the "yo-yos." *Focus on the escalator.* The escalator is the long-term reality that companies will continue to sell soap, gum, boots, coffee, toilet paper, tobacco, tires, music, books, computers, and a record amount of Star Wars movie tickets. Why will they continue to sell products? Because we keep buying them. Not only do *we* keep buying them, but the new middle class also keeps buying them.

Take a look at the increase in global demand for stuff. Every year, a new middle class comes out of India ready to buy an iPhone, and this middle class is equal to the entire population of Canada! The escalator screams that products will still be consumed and companies will still make money . . . the escalator will continue to go up.

To answer the original question . . . will the market crash? I really, really doubt it. The probabilities of a crash are not as high as the alternative. You need to start betting on optimism today and frankly, I've never met a successful pessimist.

Age 73: QVC and Adult Children

"The secret to permanently breaking any bad habit is to love something greater than the habit."

— Bryant McGill, author

I've seen it more than enough. Money is handed over to both QVC and adult children a little too carelessly. These transactions are never one-time events. They become habits and are a threat to a senior's long-term money plan.

QVC

QVC stands for Quality, Value, and Convenience. It is the forefather to Amazon and, collectively, both fill emotional gaps in peoples' lives when debit card information is transferred. Someone who is lonely, sad, or simply bored acquires a sweet chemical rush when they make a purchase. Then, it comes back again when UPS drops off the package. The feeling continues with the search of a box opener. But eventually the rush goes away, the sadness returns, and the cycle is repeated.

According to Brad Klotz, PhD, and Ted Klotz, PhD, authors of *Mind over Money*, compulsive buying afflicts one in twenty people in the US (approximately the same rate as clinical depression) and over 75 percent of compulsive shoppers are women. This compulsive spending can be as financially damaging as alcohol abuse, smoking, or compulsive eating.

Ultimately this compulsive shopping leads to piles of unopened boxes and multiple variations of blenders filling up a living-room corner. In a blink of an eye, a QVC and Amazon addict goes from being lonely to being a lonely hoarder. It never satisfies.

Adult Children

We all end up with regrets in life. Unfortunately, many parents make up for regrets with money. Somehow, they equate money with love. This is a false belief and usually prevents children from becoming responsible adults. It often robs them from the character-building opportunity of overcoming life's challenges. In a worst-case scenario, it enables someone who has poor money habits, like a "friend" who buys an alcoholic a drink to help his buddy's hand stop trembling. Yet, despite the logic, many parents, in an attempt to buy love or make up for lost time, continue to enable their adult children.

What's the solution to throwing money at QVC and adult kids?

To avoid the QVC (and Amazon) addiction, get off the sofa and engage in your community. Please recognize that you are making purchases because it feels good, not because it's a good deal. In direct language, "You are being swindled and saying thank you." If you can't avoid it altogether, minimize your purchases to one per month.

It is hard to say no to family. Especially if you are a kind and gentle person. So, give the enabled children a runway. Let them know that you will give them another three months of financial support but you cannot afford to continue to help after that. If you have trouble saying no to others, try this line: "My financial advisor said I can no longer give money." My clients have used that line and . . . it works.

Even if you have the extra cash today, you may run out of money down the road if you indulge in these two bad money habits. Protect your money outflows by recognizing the root cause of the habits so you can have healthy, authentic, long-term relationships in this season of life.

By saying no to things that are life draining, you'll be able to focus on what is important. This idea of simplification has many benefits and is something many of my clients strive for in this season of life. Simplification is the focus of our next chapter.

Age 74: Simplify

"The ability to simplify means to eliminate the unnecessary so that the necessary may speak."

— Hans Hofmann, German-born American painter

When you're living on PURPOSE, it is difficult to rest if your plate is full of distractions. Like a baby holding on fiercely to a toy, I know it will be difficult to let go of things in life, but the small price of simplicity is worth it. Below are ten things you can do to help simplify your life.

1. Downsize your home to have the most efficient use of space.

2. Pay off all consumer debt and close out credit cards, especially department store cards.

3. Avoid paying bills with checks. The process takes too much time. Set up bills on auto draft or bill pay.

4. Clean out the closets and give clothes to Goodwill.

5. Eliminate unnecessary bank accounts. Five saving accounts don't compound more than one account if the money is equal.

6. Consolidate investments.

7. Have a garage sale and give away the rest.

8. Sell real estate holdings.

9. Close a business or network marketing alliance.

10. Cancel subscriptions to magazines, vitamins, and other items you rarely use.

Identify ways to get organized so you are never wasting time looking for something.

Greg McKeown, in his book called *Essentialism*, described a monk who takes a full hour to drink a cup of tea. The monk explained:

> "Suppose you are drinking cup of tea. When you hold your cup, you may like to breathe in, to bring your mind back to your body, and you become fully present. And when you are truly there, something else is also there— life, represented by the cup of tea. In that moment you are real, and the cup of tea is real. You are not lost in the past, in the future, in your projects, in your worries. You are free from all of these afflictions. And in the state of being free you enjoy your tea. That is the moment of happiness, and of peace."

Get rid of the unnecessary so you have the opportunity to enjoy your tea, smell the roses, or spend time with the ones you love.

If you simplify, you will create blank space in your brain to think about leaving a legacy. You may even want to start leaving a little bit now. The next chapter is all about how to give it away the right way.

Age 75: Advance the Inheritance

"I alone cannot change the world, but I can cast a stone across the waters to create many ripples."

— Mother Teresa, Albanian-Indian Roman Catholic nun

There is a stark contrast between inheritance and legacy. An inheritance is the receipt of money from someone after the person dies. There are some key problems with inheritances. First, the inheritance can accentuate bad behaviors. I've worked with several lottery winners and I can assure you that when they received the money they did more drugs, drank more alcohol, and parents who already weren't getting along went from sparring to "gloves off." According to the National Endowment for Financial Education, about 70 percent of people who suddenly receive a windfall of cash will lose it within a few years.

If you want to make small problems bigger, give someone a pile of cash.

The other issue with a large inheritance is that it deprives someone of the character-building opportunity of earning it on their own. That is one of the key reasons why Warren Buffett has decided not to leave the majority of his estate to his children.

The other issue with inheritance is that people expect it. Research has suggested that many people are depending on an inheritance. If the inheritance doesn't meet the expectations, then families fight and become torn apart. Fortunately, this can be circumvented by a properly built estate plan and family meetings.

The alternative to an inheritance is a legacy. A legacy is what you leave "in" someone, not what you leave "to" someone. This might require you to advance your inheritance so that you are giving some away today. Financial Guru Ron Blue said, "Do your givin' while you're livin'!" This approach is actually much more engaging for the family and for you. You can give money away to your kids directly up to $14,000 (2017) per person each year without exceeding IRS limits. Then, you can share the joy of giving while you're still alive.

The one statement needed before signing over the check is this . . .

"Here's a gift from mom and me. No strings attached. There is one thing I would like to tell you, though. I want you to be wise with this money based on what I have taught you about money over your life. That's all I'm asking."

The main reason grandparents are afraid to advance an inheritance is because of the uncertainty of life expectancy and health care costs. Prior to advancing the inheritance, sit down with a financial advisor and discuss the probabilities of success in retirement and the likelihood of running out of money.

With a confident, educated decision and a reasonable approach, the math will tell you how much inheritance is available to advance. This is why our team at PAX Financial Group believes building a plan is so critical for retirees.

If you are caught in the next chapter's retirement trap, you are going to have a hard time making a difference in the lives of others in the way you could and should.

Age 76: Fox News and Flower Beds

"I've got a great ambition to die of exhaustion, rather than boredom."

— Thomas Carlyle, Scottish philosopher

Boredom is like cancer. It can kill you. Actually . . . it really can. In a landmark eight-decade study by Howard S. Friedman, PhD, and Leslie R. Martin, PhD, called the Longevity Project, it was confirmed that those who were bored, identified as being "without meaningful connections," died sooner.

Do you find that the meaningful connections of the past aren't that connected anymore?

Many grandparents have kids who are busy juggling life. Or, their kids are spread out across the country. Friends who used to call you up for a ball game or a dinner are growing weary and are less active.

A transition of relationships is normal.

The reality is that slowing down is a choice based on your willingness to creatively identify meaningful connections. I've seen many retirees refuse to be lonely. As a result, they have relationships, friends, and a bounce in their step. Below are a few real-life connectors who refuse to live glued to Fox News and fixing their flower beds . . .

- Brad works as an usher escorting intoxicated fans out of professional sports games.

- Dan helps out at a friend's ranch, cuts trees, fixes fences, and guards against trespassers.

- Alice goes swing dancing every Wednesday night keeping her hips active and her mind sharp.

- Norma drives to the hospital and politely listens and prays with those who are hurting.

- Jeff carves wood and sells it for a loss at local flea markets because . . . it's fun.

- Beth works at a call center—because she wants to. Caller complaints "don't bother her none."

- Jesse started a coaching business helping younger people figure out life.

What do all of these people have in common? Two things. First, they are all above age seventy and second, they have somehow found a creative way to stay connected with others. If we are honest with ourselves, there is something deep inside that desires to be involved in a community.

Spending time in a community should bring back the smile you had as a child. Don't let debt steal that smile. The next chapter is simply a chapter I couldn't avoid writing.

Age 77: Settling up Debts

"If you were born poor, it's not your mistake. If you die poor, it's your mistake."

— Bill Gates, an American business magnate

Imagine a seventy-seven-year-old widower named Robert just received the news he is terminally ill and only has a few weeks to live. He loves his kids but rarely sees them. As opposed to spending the last few days with those he loves, he decides he's going to buy a black leather jacket and a motorcycle. He's always been a rule follower, but at seventy-seven, with nothing to lose, he gets a wild hair. He gathers all his credit cards and opens a few more. About four credit cards lay in front of him next to his cold beer. The total spending limit is $60,000. "This is gonna be fun," he says out loud.

He makes a point to max out every single one of the four cards. He is going to do absolutely anything he wants. He flies where he wants. He eats without restrictions. He gambles. He gets courtside tickets to a basketball game. There are no limits to his spending until the last card is declined. Then . . . he dies.

My question: who pays the credit card bills?

His first credit card was a joint credit card with his oldest son who needed the credit to do some home repairs. The widower forgot that it was opened in a joint name. When the application was submitted, they both agreed to be equally responsible for the debt. The son is now responsible for the debt.

His second card had his daughter's name on the card as a user. But, she was not a cosigner. She wasn't responsible for making payments but dad gave her the ability to make purchases if money ever was tight, and it was a way to "build up her credit." Not being a cosigner, she doesn't have to pay the debts at dad's funeral.

Robert's second son received a phone call from one of the credit card companies a few months after his dad's death. His name was never connected to any credit card and he never figured out how they tracked him down. He reported the harassing bill collector to the Federal Trade Commission (877-382-4357) and state attorney general's office. Wisely, he never paid the credit card company; even though he was related, he wasn't responsible for paying the debt.

The youngest son was the most responsible of the family. He left the estate open for another six months, called all the credit card companies, and called all three credit reporting agencies.

After six months, the estate was closed and there was not enough miscellaneous items to sell to cover all of the credit card debts. So, MasterCard and Visa took a loss on what they couldn't collect, which was about $10,000.

A few months after the estate settled a large retirement account was identified that was left to the children equally. At first there was concern because of the outstanding balance on credit cards. Then, they remembered that life insurance and retirement accounts are generally exempt from creditors.

The point is this: have a crystal-clear understanding of who is legally obligated to pay your debts at death. Don't make this process difficult for your loved ones. Check with your attorney when you establish your will to provide direction on every single liability so there are no distractions at your funeral. Finally, make sure you have enough cash available to cover the funeral costs. You don't want the casket to be a family liability.

Debt can and should be destroyed. However, sometimes it creeps in through con artists. Let's digest this threat in our next chapter.

Age 78: Here Come the Con Artists

"Trust but verify."

— Ronald Reagan, 40th President of the United States of America

The definition of a con artist is a person who cheats or tricks others by persuading them to believe something that is not true. You may think about a con man who is selling money-printing machines, Nigerian letter scams, or fortune telling.

Many con people are sneaky. Like this . . .

Suppose you have received a phone call from an unknown, soft-spoken woman. The frantic but direct young lady on the other end of the line knows your name and is clearly connected to your family. She mentions that she's a close friend of your grandson and desperately explains that he's in a lot of trouble. He is jail in a foreign country and needs $5,000 in bail money. If you don't act quickly, he could be seriously tortured. What do you do?

Or, maybe you get a call in the evening that an international ministry urgently needs a charitable donation, otherwise the children will go hungry. Do you provide your banking instructions?

How do you handle a scary, urgent, unknown call relative to your investment portfolio, a water leak, or a rare virus on your computer? Do you provide credit card information to fix the problem?

Scammers are intelligent. You must keep your guard up. However, they are not nearly as effective as these con artists . . . family.

Most seniors are scammed by people they trust. According to the National Adult Protective Services Association, 90 percent of financial abuse is from family members or people who are trusted.

For example, a grandchild moves into grandma's home, tricks grandma to sign a power of attorney, and goes on a shopping spree. Or, often a selfish child will figure out a way to have a parent remove all other beneficiaries from life insurance policies. There are many ways close family members can steal.

The financial loss is devastating and the emotional feeling is irrecoverable. Do not let this happen to you. You must ask verification questions even with the ones you love.

If you are a senior citizen and uncertain about a financial decision, visit the Consumer Financial Protection Bureau at https://www.consumerfinance.gov/ where the goal is to make sure you are treated fairly financially. So far, they have helped 29 million people!

Make it a point in your life to always "Trust, but verify." It's too expensive to allow a con artist in your world. Consider adding the decision-making tool in the next chapter to help you make better choices.

Age 79: A Filter for Decision Making

"Decision making, like coffee, needs a cooling process."

— George Washington, 1st President of the United States of America

The last time I saw my client Jim was twelve months ago, and he was sharp as a tack. A year later, he had forgotten much of our previous detailed personal conversations. I found it odd, concerning, and frankly I was a little sad.

The decline in cognitive retention advances with birthdays. It could be seen in the inability to retain information, inability to multitask, difficulty recalling names, lack of visual perception, or poor decision-making.

We can't let this inevitable brain change impact our wallets. As we get older, we must create a process for making financial decisions. Below is a list of filter questions to answer before any financial decision is made.

1. Based on my legacy, is this the right thing to do?
2. Based on my past experience, is this a wise thing to do?
3. What is the downside and the chance that it might occur?
4. Will this be a distraction?
5. What makes me think I can beat the odds?
6. Did I get advice from a child, a friend, and a sage?
7. Did I take a breath, wait and pray (most con artists create a sense of urgency)?

8. Is this decision aligned with my goals and values?

9. Did I consider my future self and others?

10. Did I consider the indirect consequences?

Answering these questions will reduce the risk of a poor decision, financial regret, or irrecoverable misstep.

Done in a Decade
1. Processed Required Minimum Distributions
2. Considered part-time employment
3. Reconfirmed commitment to long-term investing
4. Identified spending habits
5. Simplified
6. Started a giving strategy
7. Became involved in the community
8. Revisited will and address debts
9. Was careful about relationships who ask for money
10. Created a decision-making filter

Age 80: Just-in-Case Preparation

"Before anything else, preparation is the key to success."

—Alexander Graham Bell, Scottish-born scientist and inventor

Here are ten critical rules your family must follow in the event of your death to ensure it's a time of celebration and not financial worry.

1. Get certificates. They will need to gather around fifteen copies of the death certificate. Don't rely on photocopies. Many institutions will not accept them. Also, it would be helpful to call the county clerk's office for copies of marriage certificates and birth certificates.

2. Contact the county. The county is responsible for probating the will. They have courts established to help make sure the money goes to the right place. However, if you have *wisely* hired an attorney to set up your will, then go through him/her first rather than navigating uncharted waters.

3. Contact all the financial companies. Whoever is authorized to settle the estate (also called an executor) should immediately notify the health insurance companies, life insurance companies, property and casualty companies, banks, and investment companies.

4. Stop all auto drafts. Your beneficiaries will need to watch the bank account and make sure that all auto drafts are discontinued.

5. Check past tax returns. Tax returns tell stories about income sources. They may identify items that might not have surfaced when looking in the files. Your beneficiaries should look at the last two years of tax returns. Keep in mind, they will have to file a final return as well.

6. Call Social Security. Usually Social Security knows about the death before you do. Be sure to give them a call anyway. Also, if there are other pensions coming in from the Department of Veteran Affairs or a private company, notify them quickly as well.

7. Confirm any debts. Your beneficiaries will need to contact credit card, auto loan, mortgage companies, or any other lenders. Debts will need to be paid off by the estate.

8. Check the mail. In the mail, your beneficiaries may find other financial relationships. They'll need to let the utility companies know of your death. After a little while, all mail will need to be forwarded to another address.

9. Don't do. Anyone who inherits your money or assets should not do anything with the money for a year. They will need to retitle things in their names, but the idea of spending or investing immediately could be harmful. Emotions and money don't mix. That's why lottery winners are broke.

10. Budget. It is important that anyone depending on your income revises their expenses and income sources. It is helpful to be transparent in family meetings about the new cash flow plan.

As you can tell, there will be a lot of effort by your family and specifically your executor. Asking them to do this significant job with confusion and a heavy heart is a difficult task.

Plan ahead.

You can make the above action items much smoother if you provide (a) your will; (b) a list of assets and liabilities; and (c) contacts of key professional relationships in advance. Finally, have conversations with your beneficiaries. Clearly articulate why you are leaving the estate the way you decided and how it will be facilitated. You want your family to love each other after your death, not be bitter.

Take the time and plan it with preparation and thought.

Conclusion

"Let me tell you about the rich. They are very different from you and me."

— F. Scott Fitzgerald, fiction writer

Congratulations for making it through all the ages. You have established a fresh understanding of money rooted, not just in math, but in behavior and wisdom. Having a keen awareness of how people, marketers, and markets influence our money allows us to take a step back and think about our life more rationally. Now you can be in control of decisions without these meddling influences.

Middle class money challenges will continue to get bigger, so together we must remain focused.

Right now, when our middle-class friends try to get pint-sized financial support with health care costs, we are denied based on our income level. When we apply for college financial aid, it's already handed to the needier. There isn't a trust fund to tap into or an inheritance coming our way.

This middle-class money pressure will get worse. But there is hope.

Not only is there not a harder-working group of people in the world, but the middle class cares about family. We don't view our financial situation with blame or pity, but rather with accountability and responsibility.

We're the most influential group in the world. We must acknowledge our financial status, work daily to improve our money skills, and focus on leaving our community better than we found it. Imagine what our community will look like when we reframe our money for the betterment of others. That selfless approach doesn't make us just middle class . . . it makes us rich.

PIVOT Retirement Planning™ Buckets

You have three primary objectives when you PIVOT. First, you must create consistent cash flow. Second, cash flow must increase if groceries, hotels, and movie tickets get more expensive. And finally, cash flow needs to last until your final breath.

These three objectives are slightly different than life's financial goals before PIVOTing happened. Our PREPARE (before retirement) desires were to earn a big paycheck, try not to spend it all, and invest the leftovers wisely.

Now, when we PIVOT, our desired outcome is . . . income.

A sharp businessperson knows that when he/she makes decisions there is an opportunity cost involved. The opportunity cost exists in retirement as well. For example, if you are trying to mitigate the risk of outliving your money by purchasing an annuity, you will likely find yourself struggling to keep up with inflation long-term. There isn't a perfect scenario with retirement decisions, and we'll be faced with give and takes. When presented with reasonable choices we must make unemotional fact-based decisions designed to increase the probability of having a paycheck for our entire lives whether we live to be eighty-five or 105.

By setting up the following buckets, you are putting yourself in a more advantageous PIVOT position:

1. A Comfortable Cash Operating Bucket
This money is the amount of money needed to cover regular monthly bills. It also includes the cash you prefer to keep on hand. There isn't a lot of money here. I have seen people keep $2,500 up

to $15,000 in the operating account. It should be equal to one month of expenses, so be sure to know your expenses!

2. A Supersized Emergency Fund Bucket

This money will be equal to twelve times total monthly expenses. There are three unique uses for this money: (1) acute health care needs; (2) household and car repairs; and (3) market risk. Let's unpack the market risk piece, as this is the most critical component of the supersized emergency fund. From 1825 to 2013, the market (on average) finished down 20 percent once every twenty years. So, if you live twenty to thirty years, you might experience one or two material market downturns. Most of the downturns, based on history, will be fear-driven head fakes causing most of your retired friends to make emotional decisions. That won't be you.

But, there is a number on your investment statement that will steal your sleep. Everyone has a number where they lose sleep over the stock market. If you get to that point, pause any withdrawals from your investments and live off your supersized emergency fund.

If you don't do this, you could find yourself taking money from your investments while the investments are crashing. In this case, you are "eating your seed" and will be unable to reap the reward when it returns to normal. You could be taking out withdrawal checks at a low point and no one wants to sell low. By taking money from your supersized emergency fund, rather than your portfolio, you are giving your investments an opportunity to ride the stock market back up from where it fell.

The supersized emergency fund should be stored in a money market account at the bank or a six-month CD that only penalizes earnings (not principle) if the term is broken. The only criticism of this approach is, "Could I make more money by investing it, rather than having this much cash on hand?" Yes, but by keeping a little more cash on hand than normal, you are giving yourself permission to increase risk a notch more in your other investments. You are just doing it in a very intentional way.

3. A Needs Bucket

The next form of money is not so much held in an account, but rather is in the form of paychecks. We can call this the "needs bucket." You must put pen to paper and identify all your needs in your monthly budget. This will include housing costs, food, utilities, and other items needed to survive. "Needs" are expenses that would severely impact your quality of life if they couldn't be paid. Frankly, you won't find that your income needs will change much when you retire from when you were working, so creating the budget shouldn't be too challenging. The goal is to have predicable and guaranteed resources such as social security and pensions covering 100 percent of your needs.

If your monthly needs are higher than your guaranteed resources, then you will need to fill in the gap. This is done with an annuity,* which is like a private pension (annuities are discussed at age fifty-four). Don't be preconditioned to believe annuities are bad or good. Most people have an opinion because they are oversold and expensive. However, if used for a specific income purpose, they work well.

Annuities protect us against outliving our income. There is about a one in five chance that either the sixty-five-year-old husband or, more likely the wife, will live to ninety-five. Modern medicine, safety, and sanitation are consistently extending our lives. Annuity companies absolutely hate when they continue to pay an income to someone in their nineties. We must protect our family's long-term needs by covering them completely with guaranteed income sources that will continue no matter how long we live.

4. A Wants Bucket

This account will be a diversified group of investments that has a minimum five- to ten-year track record. The group of investments will be built around your specific risk profile using modern risk assessment questionnaires. If possible, lean into a little more risk, knowing you have a supersized emergency fund account and you have your needs covered.

Then, you will withdraw a periodic check from these investments to cover the "wants" portion of your budget. Make sure you do not withdraw more than 4 percent of your portfolio annually. That is your boundary. For example, if your wants are $30,000 per year and you have $300,000, you have crossed your boundary and are now at a 10 percent withdrawal rate. This is danger zone and will cause you to run out of money. You will need to lower the withdrawal amount to stay around 4 percent.

This account will also allow you pay increases over the years as food, gas, and movie tickets go up in price. But, some of those inflation impacts are offset by declines in spending. Some research studies have concluded that the retirement inflation rate (apart from health care) is considerably less than for those in their working years. Additionally, your spending may decelerate as you get tired of traveling and the long flights become uncomfortable.

Rather than putting inflation increases on autopilot, like most people do without any real thought, reexamine annually. Update the budget, review the plan, and decide if a pay increase is needed. If not, let the pay increase keep working for you in the investment portfolio.

5. A Legacy Bucket

Let's assume that you have put together a cash flow model and evaluated all your projected income checks from now until the day you die and there is money left over. This is a blessing known as a margin of safety. Let's pick at the margin of safety a bit. What if we set aside a little money and invested it differently? For example, imagine you calculated a $250,000 margin of safety in your plan and were pleasantly surprised. What if we took $50,000 out and called it "legacy"? Because you are more likely to live twenty more years than die next week, you have a long time horizon with this money. When someone has a long time horizon with money, they are given an opportunity to be slightly more aggressive.

In this example, consider taking the $50,000 out of the plan, placing it into a liquid, diversified portfolio with slightly more risk than your other investments, and labeling it legacy. If setting aside the legacy money doesn't have a material impact on your retirement cash flow, then you have the opportunity to make the money work harder for you over the years.

How can you have confidence while PIVOTing? The answer to that question is simple to say but it takes effort to do. The answer is . . . plan.

Insurance giant Genworth completed a study and concluded that pre-retirees who have developed a plan are 74 percent more confident that their money will last a lifetime, whereas only 44 percent of plan-less people had the same confidence.

Building a plan lays a foundation of confidence and reduces the odds of making emotional financial decisions. Our team at PAX Financial Group believes this is so important that we will not engage new clients without a plan.

With a concrete strategy, you are given the opportunity to enjoy the next chapter in your life with Peace, Imagination, Vigor, Opportunity, and Time (PIVOT).

*Fixed Annuities are long term insurance contacts and there is a surrender charge imposed generally during the first 5 to 7 years that you own the annuity contract. Withdrawals prior to age 59-1/2 may result in a 10% IRS tax penalty, in addition to any ordinary income tax. Any guarantees of the annuity are backed by the financial strength of the underlying insurance company.

Q & A with the Author: The Inside Scoop on Financial Advice

Michelle Booth: What does it take to become a financial advisor?

Darryl Lyons: That's actually a more difficult question to answer than it seems. There are a lot of people who call themselves a financial advisor. A person whose primary role is to sell financial products for a commission is called a registered representative, not a financial advisor. They often work with a broker dealer who provides resources to support their business. Those same registered representatives can be financial advisors if they pass either a Series 65 or 66 exam. Then, they will be subject to the financial advice laws from either their state or the Securities Exchange Commission (SEC).

Michelle: Ok, I think I get it. When they pass that 65 or 66 exam, is that when they become a fiduciary?

Darryl: That is actually a hot topic in our industry. They could be a fiduciary, but they may not be. A fiduciary is someone who is ethically bound to act in the best interest of others. In other words, if a financial advisor does not get paid a commission or other conflicted compensation from his or her recommendations, then it is likely that the financial advisor is a fiduciary.

Michelle: Are you a fiduciary?

Darryl: Yes. We act in the best interest of our clients.

Michelle: Do you have any conflicts of interests as a financial advisor?

Darryl: Everyone has conflicts and biases, but I believe ours are reasonable. For example, we sell health insurance and Medicare to our clients. It is much more reasonable for us to be paid a commission than to charge a fee for those services. Also, the financial marketplace hasn't fully adapted to the fiduciary model yet. So, in the meantime we offer term insurance, disability insurance, long term care, and some limited annuities. Those products pay us a commission, and so we disclose that information.

Michelle: That makes sense. Are you considered fee-based then?

Darryl: Yes. We are fee-based fiduciaries.

Michelle: How do you get paid?

Darryl: When we thought about building an advice company, I thought of some of my friends. When they sit down with someone in the financial world, the questions in their minds are, "What's his angle? What's he trying to sell?" They have a hard time listening to the advice. So, we decided to have all advisors on salary at PAX Financial Group and we have disclosed potential conflicts of interest in our Advisory Agreement which helps identify and manage risk to our fiduciary duty to you. Hopefully, clients can relax, listen, and make the financial adjustments needed based on wise council.

Michelle: That's cool. I've never heard of that before. So how do clients pay for a financial advisor's services? Is it by check, credit card, bitcoin?

Darryl: Ha! No bitcoin and definitely not credit cards. We are huge fans of Dave Ramsey so that doesn't work for us. Clients pay us for two things: (1) advice and (2) to manage money. We charge a reasonable percentage to manage the money. Our fee schedule can be found on our website (www.paxfinancialgroup.com). Some advisors get paid by a check for their services.

Michelle: I remember you telling me that you guys are huge Dave Ramsey fans. What does that really mean?

Darryl: In 2005, Dave had set up something called the ELP program for investment people he recommended to the community. We were a part of that group. It has evolved to the SmartVestor program and I'm on board that system as well. Finally, I'm a part of his Investment Council. That is a select group of financial advisors across the country who provides Dave boots-on-the-ground advice. I'm honored to be a part of that group.

Michelle: Thanks so much for participating in the Q&A. Is there anything else you would like to add?

Darryl: Yes! I love what I do. Money is more than cash and currency. It plays a role in dreams and failures. It's a part of your story growing up and it's a part of mine. It will be a part of my children's story and the next generation's. I want to do my best to help make happy endings. That's what I'm called to do.

Work with the Author

If you want assistance implementing the ideas and strategies presented in this book, PAX Financial Group would be happy to help you take the next step. Darryl and his team passionately work with people all over the country who want to PIVOT with PURPOSE.

www.paxfinancialgroup.com

About the Author

Darryl Lyons is the co-founder and CEO of PAX Financial Group. PAX Financial Group was named one of Inc.com's fastest growing companies in the United States. The company is consistently recognized as one of the Best Places to Work in San Antonio according to the *San Antonio Business Journal*.

He is a Certified Financial Planner™ (CFP), Chartered Financial Consultant (ChFC), Accredited Investment Fiduciary (AIF), and a Behavioral Financial Advisor™ (BFA)

Darryl is the author of two other books, published through Morgan James Publishing: *Small Business Big Pressure* and *The Grand Money Chasm*. He is a regular contributor on Forbes.com through the Forbes Finance Council and has served as an advisor for the National Federation of Independent Business Owners (NFIB), The C12 Group, and Ramsey Solutions (Dave Ramsey).

Darryl's life mission is to help others believe in a bigger life. He wants to extend his mission internationally. Through the Admirals (a nonprofit basketball academy in Moldova), he helped establish a Eurasia character/athletic award called the Dave Robinson Award.

Being from San Antonio, Texas, Darryl has also served his military community where he played a key role in a base realignment and closure (BRAC). Afterward, Mayor Julian Castro established the Darryl W. Lyons Park at Brooks City Base.

Darryl's calling to serve others through money and business is rooted in his faith. He lives in San Antonio with his wife, Caresse, and four children, Luke, Claire, Noelle, and Lucy.

Because of his commitment to family, Darryl limits his travel. However, you are welcome to submit your speaking request to **darryl@paxfg.com**.

DISCLOSURES

Content in this material is for general information only and not intended to provide specific advice or recommendations for any individual. You should discuss your specific situation with the appropriate professional. All performance referenced is historical and is no guarantee of future results. Hypothetical examples provided are for illustrative purposes only and are not intended to represent the past or future performance of any specific investment.

The Standard & Poor's 500 Index is a capitalization-weighted index of 500 stocks designed to measure performance of the broad domestic economy through changes in the aggregate market value of 500 stocks representing all major industries. All indices are unmanaged, does not reflect deduction of fees and may not be invested into directly.

There is no guarantee that a diversified portfolio will enhance overall returns or outperform a non-diversified portfolio. Diversification does not protect against market risk.

Mutual Funds and Exchange Traded Funds (ETF's) are sold by prospectus. Please consider the investment objectives, risks, charges, and expenses carefully before investing. The prospectus, which contains this and other information about the investment company, can be obtained from the Fund Company or your financial professional. Be sure to read the prospectus carefully before deciding whether to invest.

Fixed Annuities are long term insurance contacts and there is a surrender charge imposed generally during the first 5 to 7 years that you own the annuity contract. Withdrawals prior to age 59-1/2 may result in a 10% IRS tax penalty, in addition to any ordinary income tax. Any guarantees of the annuity are backed by the financial strength of the underlying insurance company.

Rebalancing can entail transaction costs and tax consequences that should be considered when determining a rebalancing strategy.

Not associated with or endorsed by the Social Security Administration or any other government agency.

Reference the PAX Financial Group Website for additional information regarding Awards and Recognitions.
https://paxfinancialgroup.com/about-pax/awards-and-recogitions/

Investment Advisory Services are offered through PAX Financial Group, LLC.

Reference Notes

"10 Subliminal Retail Tricks you're Probably Falling For." Available at: http://fortune.com/2014/12/03/10-subliminal-retail-tricks-youre-probably-falling-for/. Accessed 11/28/2017.

"17 Facts about Warren Buffet and His Wealth That Will Blow Your Mind." Available at: http://www.businessinsider.in/17-Facts-About-Warren-Buffett-And-His-Wealth-That-Will-Blow-Your-Mind/99-of-Buffetts-wealth-was-earned-after-his-50th-birthday-/slideshow/40266709.cms. Accessed 11/28/2017.

"2013 Survey of Individual Annuity Contract Owners." Available at: https://www.annuity-insurers.org/wp-content/uploads/2013/10/2013-Gallup-Survey.pdf. Accessed 11/28/2017.

"2014 Cost vs. Value Report." Available at: http://www.remodeling.hw.net/cost-vs-value/2014/. Accessed 11/28/2017.

"2014 Real Wedding Study Statistics." Available at: http://www.prnewswire.com/news-releases/the-knot-the-1-wedding-site-releases-2014-real-weddings-study-statistics-300049675.html. Accessed 11/28/2017.

"2015 Employer Health Benefits Survey." Available at: http://kff.org/report-section/ehbs-2015-summary-of-findings. Accessed 11/28/2017.

"2017 Dalbar Quantitative Analysis of Investors Behavior." Available at https://www.dalbar.com/QAIB/Index. Accessed 11/28/2017.

"21 Shocking Statistics." Available at: http://www.sheknows.com/living/articles/1023453/what-are-the-odds-21-statistics-that-will-surprise-you. Accessed 11/28/2017.

"27 Highest-Paying Jobs That You Can Train for in 2 Years or Less."
Available at: http://www.trade-schools.net/articles/highest-paying-jobs-without-degree.asp. Accessed 11/28/2017.

"40 Must-Know Statistics about Long-Term Care." Available at:
http://news.morningstar.com/articlenet/article.aspx?id=564139. Accessed 11/28/2017.

"5 Things You Need to Know about the Sandwich Generation."
Available at: http://workplace.care.com/5-things-you-need-to-know-about-the-sandwich-generation. Accessed 11/28/2017.

"7 Features That Will Sell Your Home Faster." Available at:
http://www.kiplinger.com/slideshow/real-estate/T010-S001-features-that-will-sell-your-home-faster/index.html. Accessed 11/28/2017.

"8 Lessons from 80 Years of Market History." Available at:
http://www.marketwatch.com/story/8-lessons-from-80-years-of-market-history-2014-11-19. Accessed 11/28/2017.

"8 Things You Should Know About Sports Scholarships." Available at:
https://www.cbsnews.com/news/8-things-you-should-know-about-sports-scholarships/ Accessed 11/28/2017

"America's Shrinking Middle Class." Available at:
http://www.pewsocialtrends.org/2016/05/11/americas-shrinking-middle-class-a-close-look-at-changes-within-metropolitan-areas/. Accessed 11/28/2017.

"American's Spend the Most on Saturdays." Available at:
https://economix.blogs.nytimes.com/2009/10/30/americans-spend-the-most-on-saturdays/?_r=0. Accessed 11/28/2017.

"American's With Holiday Debt Added $986 on Average." Available at:
http://www.magnifymoney.com/blog/pay-down-my-debt/holiday-debt-survey. Accessed 11/28/2017.

"Americans Hate Their Jobs and Perks Don't Help." Available at:
http://www.today.com/money/americans-hate-their-jobs-even-perks-dont-help-6C10423977. Accessed 11/28/2017.

"Annual US Market Return Histogram." Available at:
http://amarginofsafety.com/2014/01/12/annual-us-market-return-histogram-through-2013/. Accessed 11/28/2017.

"Are you in the American middle class?" Available at:
http://www.pewsocialtrends.org/2016/05/11/are-you-in-the-american-middle-class. Accessed 11/28/2017.

"Attending Premarital Counseling Does Pay Off." Available at:
https://www.mentalhelp.net/blogs/attending-pre-marital-counseling-classes-really-does-pay-off/. Accessed 11/28/2017.

"Average Student Loan Debt in America: 2017 Facts and Figures."
Available at: https://www.valuepenguin.com/average-student-loan-debt.
Accessed 11/28/2017.

"Behavioral Finance: Theories and Evidence." Available at:
http://www.cfapubs.org/doi/pdf/10.2470/rflr.v3.n1.1. Accessed 11/28/2017.

"Best Practices for Portfolio Rebalancing." Available at:
https://www.vanguard.com/pdf/icrpr.pdf. Accessed 11/28/2017.

"Boomerang Generation." Available at:
https://en.wikipedia.org/wiki/Boomerang_Generation. Accessed
11/28/2017.

"Boomers: America's Least Engaged Employees." Available at:
https://www.google.com/amp/www.nextavenue.org/boomers-americas-least-engaged-employees/amp/. Accessed 11/28/2017.

"Chances of Disability. Me Disabled?" Available at:
http://www.disabilitycanhappen.org/chances_disability/disability_stats.asp.
Accessed 11/28/2017.

"Credit Cards Make You Spend More: Studies." Available at:
https://www.nerdwallet.com/blog/credit-cards/credit-cards-make-you-spend-more. Accessed 11/28/2017.

"Do You Really Need 10X Your Salary in Life Insurance?" Available at:
https://www.lifehappens.org/blog/do-you-really-need-10x-your-salary-in-life-insurance/. Accessed 11/28/2017.

"Does Using a Good Accountant Lower the Odds of a Tax Audit?"
Available at: http://finance.zacks.com/using-good-accountant-lower-odds-tax-audit-2854.html. Accessed 11/28/2017.

"Does Your Kid Need a Coach to Get Into College?" Available at: www.cnbc.com/id/48741222. Accessed 11/28/2017.

"Does Your State Have an Estate or Inheritance Tax? Available at: https:// taxfoundation.org/does-your-state-have-estate-or-inheritance-tax/, Accessed 11/28/2017.

"Elder Financial Exploitation." Available at: http://www.napsa-now.org/policy-advocacy/exploitation/. Accessed 11/28/2017.

"Estimating Changes in Retirement Expenditures and the Retirement Spending Smile." Available at: https://www.kitces.com/blog/estimating-changes-in-retirement-expenditures-and-the-retirement-spending-smile/. Accessed 11/28/2017.

"Financial Exploitation of the Elderly." Available at: http://www.nij.gov/topics/crime/elder-abuse/pages/financial-exploitation.aspx. Accessed 11/28/2017.

"Five Reasons 8 out of 10 Businesses Fail." Available at: https://www.forbes.com/sites/ericwagner/2013/09/12/five-reasons-8-out-of-10-businesses-fail/#6e59e3616978. Accessed 11/28/2017.

"Food-Away-from-Home." Available at: https://www.ers.usda.gov/topics/food-choices-health/food-consumption-demand/food-away-from-home.aspx. Accessed 11/28/2017.

"Forget bingo! More Americans are working part-time in retirement." Available at: http://www.investmentnews.com/article/20170506/FREE/170509961/forget-bingo-more-americans-are-working-part-time-in-retirement. Accessed 11/28/2017.

"Full Market Cycle." Available at: https://asymmetryobservations.com/definitions/full-market-cycle. Accessed 11/28/2017.

"Get rid of that debt before you retire." Available at:
http://www.usatoday.com/story/money/columnist/brooks/2015/04/22/retirem
ent-401k-debt-mortgage/25837369/. Accessed 11/28/2017.

"Getting Rich after 50." Available at: http://www.aarp.org/work/working-
after-retirement/info-2016/getting-rich-after-50.html. Accessed 11/28/2017.

"Home Improvements that Add the Most Value." Available at:
http://www.cnbc.com/id/48692031. Accessed 11/28/2017.

"How Close Do You Live to Your Grandchild?" Available at:
https://www.statista.com/statistics/241891/distance-between-us-
grandparents-and-their-grandchildren/. Accessed 11/28/2017.

"How often should Investors expect a 5% Market Correction?"
Available at: http://investing.covestor.com/2014/08/often-investors-expect-
5-market-corrections. Accessed 11/28/2017.

"How to Avoid an Audit by the IRS." Available at:
http://www.bankrate.com/finance/taxes/red-flags-that-tempt-the-tax-auditor-
1.aspx. Accessed 11/28/2017.

"How to Pay off Your Credit Cards: Three Strategies for Success."
Available at: http://money.usnews.com/money/personal-
finance/articles/2014/10/20/3-strategies-to-pay-off-your-credit-cards.
Accessed 11/28/2017.

"Investing and Emotions." Available at:
https://www.blackrock.com/investing/literature/investor-education/investing-
and-emotions-one-pager-va-us.pdf. Accessed 11/28/2017.

"Is Retirement Good for Health or Bad?" Available at:
http://www.health.harvard.edu/blog/is-retirement-good-for-health-or-bad-for-
it-201212105625. Accessed 11/28/2017.

"Job Outlook: The Attributes Employers Want to See..." Available at:
http://www.naceweb.org/career-development/trends-and-predictions/job-
outlook-2016-attributes-employers-want-to-see-on-new-college-graduates-
resumes/. Accessed 11/28/2017.

"Long-Term Care – Important Information For Women." Available at: http://www.aaltci.org/long-term-care-insurance/learning-center/for-women.php. Accessed 11/28/2017.

"Long-Term Projections for Social Security." Available at: https://www.cbo.gov/sites/default/files/111th-congress-2009-2010/reports/10-22-socialsecurity_chartbook.pdf. Accessed 11/28/2107.

"Majority in U.S. Do Not Have a Will." Available at: http://www.gallup.com/poll/191651/majority-not.aspx. Accessed 11/28/2017.

"Marriage and Divorce." Available at: https://www.cdc.gov/nchs/fastats/marriage-divorce.htm. Accessed 11/28/2017.

"Medicare Advantage (Part C) Private Health Plans." Available at: https://www.medicareresources.org/medicare-benefits/medicare-advantage/. Accessed 11/28/2017.

"Millennials Expect Raises, Promotions More Than Other Generations." Available at: https://www.shrm.org/resourcesandtools/hr-topics/talent-acquisition/pages/millennials-raises-promotions-generations.aspx. Accessed 11/28/2017.

"More College Grads Move Back Home with Mom and Dad." Available at: http://www.cnbc.com/2016/06/10/more-college-grads-move-back-home-with-mom-and-dad.html. Accessed 11/28/2017.

"New Car, New Reality: Auto Loan Borrowing Hits Fresh New Heights." Available at: http://www.cnbc.com/2016/06/02/us-borrowers-are-paying-more-and-for-longer-on-their-auto-loans.html. Accessed 11/28/2017.

"New Year's Resolution Statistics." Available at: http://www.statisticbrain.com/new-years-resolution-statistics/. Accessed 11/28/2017.

"Odds Are…" Available at: http://funny2.com/odds.htm. Accessed 11/28/2017.

"Out-of-pocket maximum/limit." Available at:
https://www.healthcare.gov/glossary/out-of-pocket-maximum-limit/.
Accessed 11/28/2017.

**"Parents Expected to Spend $245,340 to Raise a Child Born in 2013,
According to USDA Report."** Available at:
https://www.usda.gov/wps/portal/usda/usdahome?contentid=2014/08/0179.
xml. Accessed 11/28/2017.

"Peak Earnings for Men Come in Their Early 50s." Available at:
http://www.marketwatch.com/story/peak-earnings-for-men-come-in-their-
early-50s-2015-06-18. Accessed 11/28/2017.

"Plan for a Long Retirement." Available at:
https://personal.vanguard.com/us/insights/retirement/plan-for-a-long-
retirement-tool. Accessed 11/28/2017.

"Plan Your Path to College." Available at:
http://www.collegedata.com/cs/contentcontent_payarticle_tmpl.jhtml?article
Id=10064. Accessed 11/28/2017.

"Playing the Probabilities." Available at:
http://awealthofcommonsense.com/2015/11/playing-the-probabilities/.
Accessed 11/28/2017.

**"Putting Value on Your Value: Quantifying Vanguard Advisor's
Alpha."** Available at: http://www.vanguard.com/pdf/ISGQVAA.pdf.
Accessed 11/28/2017.

"Rate-of-Return analysis shows value of delaying Social Security."
Available at:
http://www.investmentnews.com/article/20140225/BLOG05/140229928/rate
-of-return-analysis-shows-value-of-delaying-social-security. Accessed
11/28/2017.

"Retirement Will Kill You." Available at:
https://www.bloomberg.com/view/articles/2013-06-11/retirement-will-kill-
you. Accessed 11/28/2107.

"Retirement, What Percentage of Salary to Save." Available at: http://www.investopedia.com/articles/personal-finance/092414/retirement-what-percentage-salary-save.asp. Accessed 11/28/2017.

"Setting the Record Straight on Asset Allocation." Available at: https://blogs.cfainstitute.org/investor/2012/02/16/setting-the-record-straight-on-asset-allocation/. Accessed 11/28/2017.

"Spending from a Portfolio: Implications of Withdrawal Order for Taxable Investors." Available at: http://www.vanguard.com/pdf/icrsp.pdf. Accessed 11/28/2017.

"Survey: Certified Divorce Analyst® (CFDA®) Professionals Reveal the Leading Causes of Divorce." Available at: https://www.institutedfa.com/Leading-Causes-Divorce/. Accessed 11/28/2017.

"The Facts on Medicare Spending and Financing." Available at: http://kff.org/medicare/fact-sheet/medicare-spending-and-financing-fact-sheet/. Accessed 11/28/2017.

"The Real Secrets to a Longer Life." Available at: http://www.apa.org/monitor/2011/12/longer-life.aspx. Accessed 11/28/2017.

"The Return on Investment for Delaying Social Security Beyond 62." Available at: https://www.onefpa.org/journal/Documents/April2015_Contributions_Rose.pdf. Accessed 11/28/2017.

"The Secret Shame of Middle-Class Americans." Available at: https://www.theatlantic.com/magazine/archive/2016/05/my-secret-shame/476415/. Accessed 11/28/2017.

"The Stock Market. A Look at the Last 200 Years." Available at: http://basehitinvesting.com/the-stock-market-a-look-at-the-last-200-years/. Accessed 11/28/2017.

"Time, Not Timing, Is What Matters." Available at: https://www.americanfunds.com/advisor/tools/client-conversations/market-timing.html. Accessed 11/28/2017.

"Top Red Flags that Trigger an IRS Audit." Available at:
https://turbotax.intuit.com/tax-tools/tax-tips/IRS-Tax-Return/Top-Red-Flags-That-Trigger-an-IRS-Audit/INF22648.html. Accessed 11/28/2017.

"Unmarried Boomers Confront Old Age." Available at:
http://s3.documentcloud.org/documents/322105/baby-boomers-confront-old-age.pdf. Accessed 11/28/2017.

"What are the Odds of Living to 100?" Available At:
http://discovertheodds.com/what-are-the-odds-of-living-to-100/. Accessed 11/28/2017.

"What Are Your Odds of Getting Your Identity Stolen?" Available at:
https://www.identityforce.com/blog/identity-theft-odds-identity-theft-statistics. Accessed 11/28/2017.

"What Average Annual Return is Typical for a Long Term Investment in the Real Estate Sector?" Available at:
http://www.investopedia.com/ask/answers/060415/what-average-annual-return-typical-long-term-investment-real-estate-sector.asp. Accessed 11/28/2017.

"What does Medicare Cover?" Available at:
https://www.medicareinteractive.org/get-answers/introduction-to-medicare/explaining-medicare/what-does-medicare-cover-parts-a-b-c-and-d. Accessed 11/28/2017.

"What Is Compound Interest?" Available at:
http://money.usnews.com/investing/articles/2017-03-22/what-is-compound-interest. Accessed 11/28/2017.

"What is the Average Annual Return for the S&P 500?" Available at:
http://www.investopedia.com/ask/answers/042415/what-average-annual-return-sp-500.asp. Accessed 11/28/2017.

"Who Itemizes Deductions?" Available at: https://taxfoundation.org/who-itemizes-deductions. Accessed 11/28/2017.

"Your Nest Is Empty? Enjoy Each Other." Available at:
http://www.nytimes.com/2009/01/20/health/20well.html?scp&_r=0. Accessed 11/28/2017.

Berger, J. *Contagious: **Why Things Catch On.*** Simon & Schuster. Reprint Edition. May 3, 2016.

Corley, T. *Rich Habits: **The Daily Success Habits of Wealthy Individuals.*** Langdon Street Press. March 1, 2010.

Frankl, V. **Man's Search for Meaning.** Beacon Press. 1 Edition. June 1, 2006.

Halvorson, H. **Succeed: How We Can Reach Our Goals.** Plume. Reprint Edition. December 27, 2011.

Kahneman, D. **Thinking Fast and Slow.** Farrer, Straus, and Giroux. 1 Edition April 2, 2013.

McKeown, G. *Essentialism: **The Disciplined Pursuit of Less.*** Crown Business. 1 Edition. April 15, 2014.

Stanley, T. and Danko, W. **The Millionaire Next Door: The Surprising Secrets of America's Wealthy**. Taylor Trade Publishing; Reissue Edition. November 16, 2010.

The Editors of Time. *TIME: **The Science of Happiness. New Discoveries for a More Joyful Life***. TIME. June 10, 2016.